Acclaim for Robin Gaby Fisher's

After the Fire

A TRUE STORY OF FRIENDSHIP AND SURVIVAL

"Honest and intimate.... A medical education and a detective story unfold within this consistently dramatic account, as Fisher joins a reporter's curiosity and objectivity to a near-familial access to the principals.... Fisher succeeds in making what might have been yesterday's news into today's inspiration."

—*Publishers Weekly* (starred review)

"A powerfully touching book... showcasing the author's superb reporting and storytelling skills.... *After the Fire* is a gut-wrenching read.... In 2001, Fisher was nominated for a Pulitzer Prize for this series but didn't win. She was robbed."

—Karen Algeo Krizman, *Rocky Mountain News*

"Unimaginably moving—readers will want to keep a box of tissues at hand—and deeply compassionate."

—Caroline Leavitt, *People*

"Fisher's reporting is meticulous.... A riveting and intimate read. That these two men survived is almost a miracle. That Fisher was there to document it is our good fortune."

—Laurie Hertzel, *Minneapolis Star Tribune*

"Fisher tells the moving story of how the two friends found their way back from near death on that horrific night."

—*New York Daily News*

"A tearjerker. . . . A tale of both tragedy and triumph."

—*NJ Savvy Living*

"A gripping story. . . . Sometimes heartbreaking but always compelling, *After the Fire* is a complicated story movingly told with honesty and clarity." —Joan Barbato, *Newark Star-Ledger*

"Robin Gaby Fisher's moving account of two college roommates' struggle to survive and then cope after they're horribly burned in the 2000 Seton Hall University dorm fire is not one of those books you can't put down. . . . In fact, you almost certainly will put this book down after every chapter or two, if only briefly, to sigh over the unimaginable pain and suffering, to dry your eyes and steady your emotions. You'll have to break from the book to douse the gruesome scenes of the deadly fire from your mind and erase disturbing details from inside the hospital burn unit. Then you'll read on, hoping against odds for a triumphant ending. . . . Fisher's newspaper-feature style translates well into a fast-paced narrative, and her meticulous research digs deeply into the night of the fire, the law-enforcement investigation, and modern medical treatment of burns. . . . If this uplifting story of courage and friendship raises any doubt for the reader, it's that Fisher seems too close to her subject at times—her portrayal of Simons and Llanos is almost too good to be true." —Don Oldenburg, *USA Today*

"Once I started reading I could not stop. . . . And then I moved into that post-reading trance that a well-told story can put you into. . . . Books like this sober you up about the fragility of life. *After the Fire* is a book you don't want to miss—and you will want to talk about it." —Bookreporter.com

After the Fire

After the Fire

A TRUE STORY OF FRIENDSHIP AND SURVIVAL

Robin Gaby Fisher

BACK BAY BOOKS
Little, Brown and Company
New York Boston London

Back Bay Books / Little, Brown and Company
Hachette Book Group
237 Park Avenue, New York, NY 10017
www.hachettebookgroup.com

Originally published in hardcover by Little, Brown and Company, August 2008
First Back Bay paperback edition, January 2010

Library of Congress Cataloging-in-Publication Data
Fisher, Robin Gaby.
After the fire : a true story of friendship and survival / Robin Gaby Fisher.—1st ed.
p. cm.
ISBN 978-0-316-06621-1 (hc) / 978-0-316-06622-8 (pb)
1. Burns and scalds—Patients—United States—Bibliography.
I. Title.
RD96.4.F47 2008
362.197'1100922—dc22 2007050621

10 9 8 7 6 5 4 3 2 1
RRD-IN

Printed in the United States of America

For Alvaro and Shawn

After the Fire

Chapter 1

Shawn Simons was a light sleeper, had been since he was *this* big. Sometimes all it took was the rustling sound of his roommate turning in bed to awaken him. Not surprisingly, the wailing fire alarm nearly shook him out of his skin.

Shawn shot up in his bed. "Not again," he said, half-angry, half-bewildered, peering at the glowing green numbers on his bedside alarm clock. It was four thirty in the morning, and the middle of one of the coldest Januarys on record in northern New Jersey. He had gotten about forty-five minutes of sleep, and his toughest class was scheduled to begin in just four hours.

The dorm had been rowdier than usual after Seton Hall's surprising win over its Big East basketball rival, Saint John's, and students had celebrated into the early morning hours with parties all over campus. Shawn had dropped in to one or two of the spontaneous gatherings, then watched a movie with his roommate before finally turning in. Sitting up now, he saw that his dorm room window glittered with frost, and a family of icicles hung from the eaves outside. As usual, his room was cold. Shivering under his heavy woolen blanket, he lay back down and hoped for quiet to return, but the alarm continued to shriek.

In the four months that Shawn had lived in Boland Hall, the freshman dormitory at Seton Hall University, the fire alarm had been pulled at least once a week. It had happened so often during December finals that he finally went home to nearby Newark to study rather than risk the constant distraction. What irked him most was that it was usually another student playing a prank. What kind of person got his kicks by scaring everyone else? He didn't understand it.

And this time was probably no different. Maybe he would just wait it out and pray he didn't get caught by the dorm adviser. Shawn shut his eyes, trying to encourage sleep, but his mind immediately started to race. Seton Hall had a rule, right there in black and white in the student handbook: if you were caught skipping a fire drill, the fine was a hundred dollars, no ifs, ands, or buts. His mother had worked two jobs all her life so that he and his older sister, Nicole, could wear decent clothing and live in a comfortable apartment. It was because of her sacrifices that they had a better life than most of the other kids who lived on their ragged city block. How could he risk her having to pay money she didn't have?

Willing himself out from under warm covers, Shawn climbed out of bed and stumbled over to his sleeping roommate, Alvaro Llanos. He had only met Alvaro four months earlier, when they were assigned to room together on the third floor of Boland Hall. Alvaro was shy and quiet, and they shared little in common except for their age and their love of baseball, and even then, they rooted for rival teams—Shawn for the Yankees, Alvaro for the Mets. Nevertheless, they had hit it off. Alvaro often told people that on freshman orientation day, with students swarming around everywhere, he had pointed to Shawn and told his parents, "I think he's going to be my roommate." Sure enough, when they walked into room 3028, there sat Shawn, gabbing on his cell phone. It was meant to be.

"Alvaro!" Shawn said, shaking his bigger, bulkier roommate by the shoulder.

He barely stirred. Alvaro slept through everything.

One hundred dollars, Shawn thought, and tried again.

"Come on, Al," he said impatiently. "There's a fire drill. We have to get dressed. Get up!"

"¿Qué pasa?" Alvaro asked sleepily. Sometimes, when he was drowsy, he unintentionally reverted to Spanish, the language his Colombian-born parents spoke in their home.

"It's a fire drill, Al. Let's go. We have to go outside."

Shaking off sleep, Alvaro finally dragged himself out of bed. In the dim glow of a single forty-watt light, the roommates pulled on their jeans and shirts from the night before. They slipped on their socks and sneakers, not bothering to tie the laces, then grabbed their winter jackets.

Shawn was one step ahead of Alvaro when he pulled open the door and stopped short. A fierce wave of blistering heat slammed him backward, and a blast of sour-tasting black smoke stuck in his throat, choking him.

"Oh my God," Shawn whispered, his skin prickling with fear. "My God, Al! This is real."

The hallway was pitch dark and Shawn couldn't see anything. It was eerily quiet, except for the shrill bursts of the fire alarm. Dropping to his knees, he took a deep breath and crawled to the right, into the blackness, toward the elevator he always took down to the first floor of the six-story dormitory. He glanced back just in time to see Alvaro swallowed up by the smoke. In a building of six hundred students, Shawn suddenly felt alone, even though he figured Alvaro must be right on his heels. He pressed blindly forward on his hands and knees, squeezing his eyes tighter, his chest about to explode from holding his breath too long. The heat was punishing. He felt as if he were crawling on red-hot coals, and his palms kept sticking to the melting floor tiles. *Hell must feel like this,* he thought.

Then it got hotter.

Shawn ripped at his clothes, throwing his jacket ahead of him to crawl over. He pulled off his sweatshirt and stuffed it in his mouth. He crawled, faster, feeling his way along the hallway wall, trying to find the elevator, feeling for a way out. He wondered if Alvaro was still behind him. He opened one eye long enough to see that his glasses were caked solid with black soot. Shawn tried to wipe the soot away. He still hadn't seen flames, just smoke, but now he smelled burning flesh. Could it be his? *Please, God,* he prayed. *It can't end this way. Not here. Please, not now. I'm just a kid. And what will my mother do if I die?*

Scrambling forward, Shawn fought the urge to gulp air. His lungs felt like they were on fire. Tiny stars darted in the spaces behind his closed eyes. Shawn could sense a dark curtain descending, unconsciousness creeping into his head. He willed himself on, on, on. *Wait.* Was that an opening? Shawn crawled left, toward a gush of cold air. The smoke was thinner there and he could see he was now in someone else's dorm room. No one else was there. A window was open and the screen was gone. *Did someone jump out?* he wondered. Rising to his feet, he leaned out the window. He realized he was at the back of the building. He looked down. It was a long way to the ground. He devoured a mouthful of the fresh, frigid air, and his lungs felt like rubber bands ready to snap.

"Please!" Shawn cried in the silent night. "Somebody help me! I don't know how to get out!"

The sky was navy blue, and the dark campus was strangely still. *What's the use?* he thought. *Nobody hears me. Nobody's there.* Sinking to the floor, he began to pray again.

The Lord is my Shepherd; I shall not want.
He maketh me to lie down in green pastures:
He leadeth me beside the still waters.
He restoreth my soul:
He leadeth me in the paths of righteousness for His name's sake.

Yea, though I walk through the valley of the shadow
of death,
I will fear no evil:
For thou art with me.

Then out of the darkness came a quiet voice.

"Crawl left out of the door. An exit will be on your right."

Obeying the faceless command, Shawn crawled back out into the heat and smoke. It was his only chance, and he had to take it. He felt around with his right hand and, as promised, found another open door. Pushing through it, he slid on his belly down one, then two flights of stairs. He landed at the bottom with a loud thud and felt almost giddy. *I'm alive,* he thought. *I'm alive.* He pushed himself up and stumbled outside into the bitter night. Falling on his knees on the hard, frost-covered ground, he looked at his hands. They were cold. And they were smoking.

On the front side of Boland Hall, Angie Gutierrez awakened to the sound of banging on her dorm room door. Alvaro, she thought, hearing the shrill sound of the fire alarm. Angie and Alvaro had been high school sweethearts. They had met in honors physics class at John F. Kennedy High School in the city of Paterson, New Jersey, at the beginning of their senior year and planned to be together forever. Alvaro was dark and handsome, with a quiet kind of charisma, and all of the girls wanted him. But he had eyes only for Angie, a bubbly girl with a ponytail, and they were the envy of the freshman dorm. They took the same classes, studied in each other's room, and worked side by side in the campus computer lab. The frequent middle-of-the-night fire drills had become another chance to be together, and over the months, they had developed a routine: when a fire alarm sounded, Angie waited in her first-floor room for Alvaro to come down from the third floor, and then they went outside to wait out the drill together.

"Wake up!" Angie called to her roommate as she pulled on her robe and sneakers and rushed to the door to greet her boyfriend. Instead, she found two of Alvaro's friends standing there wearing only boxer shorts, undershirts, and worried looks.

"Angie!" they cried. "Come quick! This is a real fire. We have to get out."

"Where's Alvaro?" Angie asked.

Faisal Ali and Altaf Plaique lived next door to Shawn and Alvaro in an adjoining room on the third floor. They said that in their panic to get away from the fire, they'd forgotten to look for their neighbors. There hadn't been time to do anything but flee, and the smoke had been so thick that they ran right into a wall before they backtracked and found the stairway. "C'mon," Faisal said, pulling Angie out of her room. "We'll find them outside."

Angie grabbed her cell phone from the table beside her bed and punched in Alvaro's dorm room number. Busy. She called his cell phone. No answer. It had only been an hour since he had walked her down to her room after they'd watched the movie *Armageddon* with Shawn. She'd been frightened by the movie, and Alvaro, being Alvaro, had comforted her until she felt safe enough to go to sleep.

Where is he? she wondered, running toward the first-floor stairway.

"Alvaro!" she cried, hoping to see him coming down the stairs. "Al! Where are you?"

The boys rushed after her and tried to pull her away, but Angie stood firm.

"Go on!" she ordered them. "Get out! I'm waiting here for Al."

Angie had barely finished her sentence when out of the smoke came a grisly apparition. A boy ran and then tumbled down the stairs toward her. His clothes were burning off his body, and he was hitting himself, trying to beat out the flames. Other students ran after him, tossing coats and sweaters in a desperate attempt to smother the blaze. A screaming girl pulled a fire extinguisher off the wall and sprayed the boy, covering him with fine white powder. He looked like a monster in a horror movie.

As the burning boy stumbled forward, Angie could see he was disoriented and running aimlessly. She stood there, watching him approach her, too stunned to move. The boy moved closer and she felt her legs start to buckle.

He was charred black.

Terrified, Angie no longer resisted when Alvaro's friends tugged at her arm. They pulled her down the hallway toward Boland Hall's front entrance. Before she ran outside, Angie stopped and turned to look one last time. She saw the boy stagger to a couch in the lobby and slump into it. His clothes were in tatters, and he was moaning that he was cold. So cold.

Angie couldn't breathe. Momentarily frozen in place, she stood there and sobbed. Then she joined the others and rushed outside into the frigid night, leaving the boy there. She had really wanted to help him, but she needed to find Alvaro.

"Where the hell is he?" she screamed.

Outside Boland Hall, help was beginning to arrive. Brian O'Hara was one of the first rescuers on the scene. Driving through the university's black iron gates, the rookie paramedic found the campus in chaos. The sights and sounds were hellish. Smoke poured from open windows, and students leaned out, pleading for help. Pajama-clad kids milled around outside, many walking barefoot on the frozen ground. One girl wore teddy bear slippers. Tears had left deep tracks in the black soot that caked her face.

"What the hell is going on out there?" the dispatcher shouted over the radio. O'Hara had no answer.

The paramedic jumped out of the ambulance and walked among the wandering students. He tried to take it all in: A boy whose shorts had melted onto his skin. A girl slapping at her smoking hair. Students screaming for missing friends.

"I had God's arms around me," one dazed-looking boy said as he walked toward O'Hara. "That's why I got out."

"There's a boy over there that's burned real bad," O'Hara heard someone say. A few feet away, a student in a police car was kicking at the back windows. An officer had found him wandering outside and locked him in the back of the squad car while he ran back into the burning building, looking for other students. The boy felt trapped and was trying to force his way out. Soon he was in the back of O'Hara's rig.

"What's your name?" O'Hara asked.

"Shawn," he said, gasping for breath.

"How do you feel, Shawn?"

"Scared," he said.

Shawn seemed alert and lucid, but it was obvious to O'Hara that he was gravely injured. His eyes were engorged, and his face bubbled with leathery blisters. His nose and his mouth were packed with soot, and every breath he took seemed to be a struggle. O'Hara clamped an oxygen mask over his face. As he did so, he glimpsed Shawn's hands. O'Hara had never seen anything like them. The skin looked like burned tissue paper, ashily shedding off, and it was smoking. From his training, O'Hara knew Shawn's hands were still burning beneath the charred outer layers of skin.

O'Hara doused Shawn's hands with water from a bottle, and they sizzled—like a raw egg hitting a hot frying pan. The medic nearly vomited from the sickening smell. He strapped Shawn onto a gurney, rolled him into the back of his rig, and took off for the hospital, red lights flashing, sirens blaring, not at all sure his young passenger would survive the ride.

O'Hara knew exactly where to go. Saint Barnabas Medical Center had the best burn unit in the state; it was one of the best on the entire East Coast. The worst burn cases were taken there, and the hospital, located in Livingston, New Jersey, was only a short ride from Seton Hall. The trip usually took fifteen minutes. At that time of the morning, with no traffic on the roads, O'Hara made it in seven.

Judging by all the lights inside, the emergency room was already in full swing. O'Hara wasn't surprised. Two nurses met him as he pulled up to the emergency room portico.

"What do you have?" one of them asked.

"The kid's in bad shape," O'Hara announced, swinging open the back doors of the ambulance.

"Are there others?" the nurse asked him.

"We have multiple casualties," O'Hara replied.

The nurses helped roll the gurney off the ambulance and onto the ground. O'Hara looked at his young charge. The boy's eyes had swollen to slits.

"Please don't leave me," Shawn cried.

"You're in the best hands now, buddy," O'Hara said, as a team of men and women in scrubs descended on the boy. O'Hara willed himself not to cry.

At the same moment, a second ambulance pulled up. The driver, a South Orange police officer who had commandeered an ambulance when the first report of a fire came in, said the boy inside had been found lying on a couch in the front lobby of the burning building. He was still conscious but barely alive. Maureen Warren, a veteran of the hospital's mobile intensive care unit, rushed to the patient's side. His face was charred black, and chunks of his ears had been burned off. He was almost naked and was shivering uncontrollably. Warren was a kindly woman. She had seen her share of tragedy during her twenty-year career, but she never got used to the kids. She looked into the boy's brown eyes and saw sheer terror. When she leaned in close to comfort him, she could feel the heat radiating from his burned skin. She spoke gently, the way she would to one of her own children, thinking that hers could be the last voice the boy ever heard.

"What is your name, son?" she asked.

"Alvaro," he whispered, a single tear dripping from the corner of his eye. "My name is Alvaro."

The boy on the floor was dead. Two firefighters crouched over his lifeless body. John Frucci had heard someone say they found the young man sprawled just inside a dorm room door. The firefighters had pulled him into the hallway to try to resuscitate him. Taking turns, they blew air into his mouth and pounded on his chest, then started all over again, hoping to restart his heart, encouraging him. *Come on, son. Come back to us. C'mon now. Come on back . . .*

It was no use. As the smoke swirled around them, one of the firefighters, then the other, picked themselves up off the floor. Eighteen-year-old John Giunta was beyond saving. The firefighters took a sooty blanket and, sobbing like babies, gently covered his body.

Frucci got a lump in his throat. He felt almost as bad for the firefighters as he did for the boy. How many times had he watched rescue workers fight valiantly to save a life when it was already too late? It made him both sad and proud.

As the on-call investigator for the Essex County prosecutor's office, Frucci had been one of the first officials on the scene, thirty minutes after the call came in. Frucci was thirty-one years old, but he'd been investigating fires for four years and had already earned a reputation as one of the best in his field. The South Orange fire chief had briefed him outside Boland Hall. *Possible fatalities,* the chief had said. *Dozens of students injured.* Most of them were already gone, whisked away to area hospitals by a fleet of ambulances a few minutes earlier.

Frucci was horrified by what he found inside. The third floor looked like a dark, smoldering cave. As he walked a few steps down the hall from where Giunta's body was found, looking for more victims, the air suddenly got hotter, and it stank of burned flesh, the stench so hard hitting that Frucci's head flew back. There was no mistaking the odor, and you never got used to it. He gagged and then walked a few more steps toward the heat and the smell.

Frucci stopped short. In front of him were the blackened corpses of two boys. Both had assumed what professionals call a pugilistic attitude. People who burned to death were often discovered in this bizarre position, lying with their knees bent and their arms held upright like a boxer's at the beginning of a prize fight.

Frucci looked around. He guessed that he was in the student lounge and that this was the place where the fire had started. Three couches smoldered, and the carpeting was melted like wax into the cement floor. It had obviously been an intensely hot blaze. The building's cinder-block frame had held in the heat, and the temperature inside was still smothering. Frucci wiped the perspiration from his face. Ceiling tiles, still glowing red hot, were scattered where they had fallen. The walls were burned black, and electrical wires dangled like snakes from the cavity beyond the scorched ceiling. *A holocaust,* he thought.

Through the smoke, Frucci saw a man dressed in black approaching. He walked slowly, tentatively. Monsignor Robert Sheeran was the president of Seton Hall University. Frucci knew him right away. As a child, Frucci had served as Sheeran's altar boy.

Sheeran had a commanding presence, but now he looked old and ghostlike. Walking through the wreckage, he went to each of the dead students, knelt down next to him, said a prayer over his body, and blessed him. Without speaking, he then turned and walked away.

"Where's the medical examiner?" Frucci asked a police officer. "We need to have the bodies taken away so we can start figuring out what happened here."

Chapter 2

The sound of the telephone sliced through the predawn darkness. Hani Mansour grabbed it on the first ring.

"What is it?" he mumbled without saying hello.

No matter how deep his sleep, the fifty-three-year-old director of the Saint Barnabas burn unit always answered the phone before the first ring finished. It was a habit he had developed when his son, Nicholas, was a baby and slept in a bassinet beside his bed.

The phone rang so often in the middle of the night that his wife, Claudette, didn't even hear it anymore.

"This is what we have," the voice on the other end said. "There's been a fire at Seton Hall. I'm hearing at least eight to ten victims. All young kids."

Chris Ruhren was in charge of the burn nurses at Saint Barnabas. She was blithe and smart and she had been treating burns longer than Mansour. They had a strong mutual respect for each other. As Ruhren continued to fill him in with the few details she knew, barely taking a breath between words, Mansour recognized the surge of adrenaline he himself felt every time his unit was about to be put to the test.

"I'm leaving now," he said, hanging up the phone.

Claudette stirred.

"What's up?" she asked sleepily.

"There's a fire at Seton Hall," Mansour said.

Claudette Mansour worked alongside her husband in the burn unit, managing the administrative work he so disliked. He had grown the unit from its infancy, and she had helped nurture it into the respected, state-of-the-art burn center it now was. As her husband threw on the same gray slacks and blue striped button-down shirt he had worn the day before, she switched on the TV in their bedroom. The New York stations were all reporting the fire, but the details were sketchy. A building on the South Orange campus was on fire. No word of casualties yet. Claudette shivered. She thought about their son, Nicolas, who had left home four months earlier to begin his freshman year at American University in Washington, D.C. Hani was so determined that their only child never be burned that he had devised a home escape plan when Nicolas was an adolescent and made him practice it regularly. Just recently they had talked about sending him an escape ladder to keep in his dorm room, the kind they kept under their own bed.

"I'll see you later," Claudette said as her husband rushed out the door.

"It could be a long day," he said.

Daylight had yet to break when Mansour jumped into his ancient red Jeep Wrangler and began the two-mile trip to the hospital. There was hardly time to think on the five-minute drive, but he reassured himself that he could handle whatever he found there. He had treated burns from Beirut to Baltimore to Fort Sam Houston, Texas, and he was confident that he had probably seen worse than what lay ahead of him. As the hospital came into view, he said the prayer he often said on the way to an emergency: "God help us to help them."

At Newark International Airport, Christine Simons had scanned her last package on the overnight shift at Federal Express when a friend from the neighborhood called.

"The radio is reporting a fire at Seton Hall," he said.

"Oh my God," she cried. "Are any of the children hurt?"

"They're not saying much on the news," he said.

The Simonses' apartment was less than a mile and two traffic lights from the boundary separating Newark from the leafy suburb of South Orange and the Seton Hall University campus. Shawn could easily have commuted to classes, but Christine had encouraged him to make the most of his college experience by living in the dorm. At first, Shawn had been homesick, but his second semester had started off well and he had adjusted to campus living. Still, he ran home every chance he got, to join his mother shopping or just hang out talking. Christine and Shawn were unusually close.

Shawn had picked up much from his mother, but Christine considered her optimism to be her greatest gift to her son. Both said things such as, "Everything will be all right," and "Every day is a good day," and "God will take care of it." And they believed it.

I'm sure the fire is out and Shawn is on his way home right now to tell me the story, Christine said to herself as she drove a little faster than usual out of the airport parking lot.

But Shawn wasn't there when Christine got home, and he wasn't answering his cell phone, so she got back in her car and drove to Seton Hall. When she got close, she saw a cavalcade of emergency vehicles, their flashing red lights bouncing off trees and buildings. A guard at the gatehouse held up his hand.

Christine stopped the car and rolled down her window.

"My son lives on campus, and I want to know if any of the children are hurt," she said.

"Sorry, ma'am, I can't let you in. You'll have to go to police headquarters for information," the guard said, turning his back on her.

Christine pulled over to the side of the road, wondering what to do.

Just then, a fire truck roared up to the guardhouse. Christine jumped out of her car and ran through the gate just as the fire truck passed through. She sprinted across the grass, up a set of stairs, and down a long sidewalk toward Boland Hall. The closer she got, the more anxious she felt. She passed injured youngsters in pajamas and T-shirts, crying and consoling one another. She searched the sea of faces, looking for Shawn. "At least one is dead," she overheard a fireman say.

Someone tapped on her shoulder.

"Aren't you Shawn's mom?" a sobbing girl asked.

"Yes, baby," Christine answered, patting the girl's long, wavy hair.

"I'm Alvaro's girl, Angie. Remember me?"

The two had met two days before. It was the Martin Luther King Jr. holiday and Shawn had no classes. "Pick me up, Mom. We need to go shopping," he had said when he called Christine at home that morning. When she arrived at the dorm, Angie was in the room with Alvaro, and Shawn had introduced them.

"Of course I remember you," Christine said.

"I can't find Alvaro or Shawn," Angie cried. "They're not answering their phones, and no one saw them come out of the building."

Christine's hands tingled and she felt almost woozy. She knew when her blood pressure was rising, and it was racing now. A student was dead—she had heard the fireman say it—and her son was missing.

Looking skyward, Christine saw smoke pouring from the third-floor windows, the floor where Shawn and Alvaro lived. *Shawn, where are you?* she wondered, trying to keep herself calm. The thought that something bad had happened to her only son, a boy she worshipped, was not a notion Christine was willing to entertain.

"Come with me," she said, leading the crying girl by the hand. "Let's check the hospital. Maybe they went there to help a friend." That was exactly the sort of thing her Shawn would have done.

Hani Mansour parked his Jeep at the curb outside the emergency room and walked quickly inside. It was 5:45 A.M. Normally this was the slowest time of day in the ER, but now it was swarming with wounded kids. Mansour was five feet four inches tall and he tended to be on the plump side, except when one of his endless fad diets happened to be going well. The twinkle in his eye betrayed his mischievous spirit, and he had an infectious, high-pitched laugh. He loved his own practical jokes. But when it came to treating patients, he was all business. And when it came to burn emergencies, there was always a sense of relief when Mansour and his team took over. The emergency room staff was reassured by his presence.

Mansour looked around and realized the biggest crisis in the burn center's history was breaking around him.

Within minutes of Mansour's arrival in the ER, his staff began filtering downstairs from the burn unit. Theirs was considered by many to be the toughest job in the hospital. It took a special person to treat burn patients. The work was both physically and emotionally draining. A single session in the tank room, cleaning and debriding a patient's burns, took brute strength and a strong stomach. Long, grueling days, hour after hour of witnessing unspeakable agony and suffering, and too many sad stories to remember were all part of the job. The worst cases were impossible to forget: A couple who had stood by helplessly as all of their children burned up in a house fire. A five-week-old baby whose hands had to be amputated after his father had held them under boiling water to stop him from crying. Sometimes a generous glass of wine or two at the end of a day was the only remedy for the pressure. Sometimes there was no remedy at all.

The overnight shift had already put in thirteen hours when the call came from the ER, and the morning shift was arriving early, having heard the first news reports. Judging from what he was seeing, Mansour knew that he would need every available member of his team.

Alvaro Llanos, in trauma room 1, was the most critical patient. Nurses wrapped him in blankets as he babbled incoherently and gasped for breath. At first glance, they hadn't been able to tell if he was covered in black soot or charred midnight. His arm was so badly burned that just putting in an intravenous line was nearly impossible.

Alvaro's airway was clogged with soot, and he was coughing up frothy sputum. In quick order, he was paralyzed with a potent muscle relaxant and sedated with the liquid tranquilizer Versed. An endotracheal tube was pushed through his mouth and down his windpipe to stop his throat from swelling closed, and an IV line was thrust into his groin to deliver a critical saline solution through his veins to keep him from going into burn shock. A second and third IV line carried a steady trickle of morphine and Versed into his bloodstream to dull the deep, relentless pain of his catastrophic burns. The dosage exceeded that which was normally given to dying patients. There was not one moment to spare. One nurse jotted down the boy's vital signs on a pant leg of her blood-spattered scrubs rather than take the time to start a chart.

Just a few feet away from his roommate, on the other side of the curtain, Shawn, still conscious, fought for every breath. His lungs, burned and clogged with mucus and soot, were closing fast. In a second, the situation had become desperate. There was no time for sedation. A breathing tube was jammed down Shawn's throat. Blood spurted out of his mouth: the tube had stabbed his esophagus.

Shawn began to gag violently. His scorched scalp had pared back from the searing heat; the skin there was peeling off in sheets. Shawn's eyes were swollen almost completely shut and he didn't know what was happening to him. Terrified, he thrashed around so wildly that two nurses and two medical residents could not keep him from moving.

"Norcuron," Mansour called to one of his nurses.

While the residents held Shawn down, the nurse jabbed a hypodermic needle into his buttocks. The drug worked like a stun gun. Within seconds, he was still.

But the drug had done nothing to quiet his fear.

Chapter 3

In the waiting room, parents searched frantically for their children. Word had begun to filter out that students had died in the fire and that dozens of others were seriously hurt.

Sue Manzo, a burn nurse, was assaulted with questions as she made her way through the crowd outside the ER. Dozens of injured students were jammed into the waiting area, and worried-looking adults spilled over onto the sidewalk outside.

Can you find out if my son is in there?

My daughter is missing.

How many children are burned?

Did any of the students die?

Can someone please tell us what's going on?

Manzo wished she could offer some comfort, but there was no time for talk. When the charge nurse had called her at home, less than an hour earlier, she had told Manzo they were expecting dozens of injured students. Manzo knew that every minute counted. As soon as she had hung up the phone, she had jumped into her clothes, brushed her teeth, pulled her hair back in a ponytail, and then driven at breakneck speed toward the hospital, running every red light she encountered.

"Someone will be out shortly to update you," she said, brushing by everyone.

Passing the nurses' station, Manzo heard the receptionist on the telephone. "No, sir, I'm sorry. I can't tell you if your son is here. I don't have any information yet. You'll have to call back." She wondered if it was the same father she had just taken a call from upstairs, in the burn unit, on the way to her locker. The poor man was beside himself with worry. He said he lived more than an hour away and he hadn't been able to reach his son by phone. All Manzo had been able to tell him was the same thing the receptionist had said: "I'm sorry, sir. You'll have to call back."

Bursting through the doors to the triage area, Manzo headed for one of the curtains. A badly burned boy held out his hand, and she grabbed it. "My roommate," he whimpered. "He was right behind me. You've got to tell me he's okay. Please tell me he's okay." The boy opened his other hand. He was clutching a golden cross on a chain. "Please give this to my mother," he said.

Manzo had witnessed indescribable horrors during her eight years as a burn nurse. She had cradled burned babies in her arms, rocking them like newborns, until they finally, mercifully, passed away. This was going to be right up there with the worst, she thought, taking the medal from the boy.

"I promise I'll give it to her," she said.

"Please don't leave me," the boy cried. "I'm so scared. If I die before my mom gets here, will you tell her I love her?"

"I'm not going anywhere, sweetie," she said.

Christine Simons had arrived at the hospital expecting to see her son in the waiting room. On the ride there, she had imagined walking in and seeing Shawn, draped in a sheet, asking to go home. In her daydream, when she called his name, he would run into her arms and reassure her: *Everything's okay, Mom. I'm fine. Really, I am.* But all Christine saw when she got there were other people's injured children and other parents desperate for information. Her ex-husband, Kenny, was among them.

"Where's Shawn?" he asked breathlessly, rushing to Christine's side.

"We need to find him," she said.

The couple had divorced when their son was four, but they were always civil to each other for the sake of Shawn. Kenny had remarried and had other children. He hadn't kept up with Shawn the way he should have, and their relationship was strained. Now he wondered what he would do without him.

Kenny had also been working the night shift, at a plastics factory five miles from Seton Hall, when he heard about the fire on a co-worker's portable radio. He had driven straight to the university, driven right through the open gates, ignoring the waving security guard. "Has anyone seen my son?" he cried as he ran around the parking lot outside Boland Hall, frantically searching for Shawn. "My son's name is Shawn Simons." Someone said several students had been taken to Saint Barnabas. Kenny was so distraught by the news, he forgot where he had parked his car. Eventually he located it and raced to the hospital.

"My son's name is Shawn Simons," Christine said when the receptionist looked up from her desk.

Christine was a diminutive woman with a gentle face and a voice that tinkled. Sometimes people initially mistook her pleasing presence for softness, but when she needed to be, she could be hard as a diamond.

The hospital wasn't giving out any information yet, the receptionist said, politely dismissing her.

Christine knew Shawn was there; she didn't know how she knew, but she could feel it, physically, and she knew he needed his mother.

"My son needs me," she said, persisting.

"Just a minute," the receptionist replied, disappearing behind the swinging doors that separated the waiting area from the ER.

When it came to doses of reality, emergency room nurses and burn nurses had very different philosophies. ER nurses figured that if a patient was going to die, it was better for his relatives to know what to expect. Shawn, they concluded, had a one-in-three chance of dying. The

ER nurses were inclined to let his parents in to see just how badly he'd been burned. But the burn nurses approached things more gently; they wanted to spare relatives the trauma of seeing their loved one at least until the carnage from his injuries was cleaned up. For now, the burn nurses held sway.

A moment later, an ER nurse walked into the reception area.

"Your son is inside," she said, standing toe-to-toe with Christine. "He is being treated, and I promise I'll come and get you as soon as we're done."

An hour passed, with nothing for Christine to do but watch other frantic parents beg for information about their children. She felt a banging in her head. She thought it might explode if she had to sit there much longer, wondering about Shawn.

Finally the nurse returned.

"Come with me," she said to Shawn's parents.

The nurse walked past the first curtain behind the swinging doors and pulled open the second. A boy lay there in a bloody bed.

Christine and Kenny simultaneously gasped. The boy looked nothing like their child. His face was not coffee-colored and smooth, but red and leathery and grotesquely swollen to nearly twice its normal size. And his hands . . . Christine had always said Shawn had such handsome hands. But this boy's hands were scorched a charcoal black and inflated like balloons.

"Shawn?" Christine said, her voice weakened to a whisper. Shawn's eyes were partly open, but he didn't seem able to see. Christine waded through the canopy of tubes and lines connected to his body and touched his head. A clump of his black hair fell onto the white pillow. She clasped her hands to her face. Shawn's curls were his pride and joy. He used to boast that he had the best hair at University High School in Newark—even better than most of the girls'. Now those ringlets lay in ruins around his burned, bloated face.

Christine swooned and reached for the edge of the bed to steady herself. Kenny caught her before she fell to the floor. A nurse pushed a chair under her and then wrapped a blood pressure cuff around her upper arm. Christine's blood pressure was dangerously high, 173 over 113. "She's always had high blood pressure," Kenny said. Suddenly, there was a team of people in green scrubs over Christine.

Are you having any chest pain? Jaw pain? Pain in your arm? Is there tightness in your chest? Do you have shortness of breath? Nausea?

"I'm feeling a little dizzy, and I have a terrible headache, but that's all," Christine said.

"Put her to bed," an emergency room doctor said.

"No," Christine cried. "My son needs me. I have to be there when he wakes up. If he wakes up and I'm not there, he'll be afraid. He'll think something's happened to me if I'm not there."

"Right now you have to take care of you," the doctor

said, refusing to budge. "Your son could be asleep for a very long time."

Two floors up, in the burn intensive care unit, a group of nurses prepared the treatment room for the onslaught of injured students. The burn unit expected twelve new admissions from the ER—as many as there were beds in the burn ICU, which was already full to capacity. The staff called the treatment area the tank room; patients called it the torture chamber.

The tank room was divided into two treatment areas separated only by an opaque plastic curtain. As usual, the thermostat was set at a muggy ninety degrees to protect patients, who no longer had healthy skin for protection, from getting a chill. Manzo was working on one side of the curtain when Alvaro was wheeled in on a stretcher to the other side. The smell of his burning flesh preceded him. Manzo winced. No matter how many patients you treated, that was something you never got used to. A team of doctors and nurses, all dressed in green scrubs and white masks, with only their different-colored clogs distinguishing them, converged on Alvaro. A booster shot of morphine was pushed into his bloodstream through an IV line, and Mansour and his team of surgeons went to work assessing his injuries. Mansour shook his head as he scanned the boy's body with his eyes. This child had suffered grave burns. The odds of survival were against him: Mansour estimated that Alvaro had a 30 percent chance of living, and even if they pulled off a miracle, his life would be nothing like it had been.

Catastrophic third-degree burns covered the upper half of Alvaro's body, and he was slowly suffocating from not being able to pull air into his smoke-clogged lungs. His torso had puffed up so dramatically that his circulation was compromised. If something wasn't done quickly to relieve the pressure, blood wouldn't be able to flow to his hands and they would have to be amputated.

The doctors performed a tracheotomy, cutting a hole in Alvaro's windpipe, and hooked him up to a respirator to breathe. An emergency escharotomy—an incision from his shoulders to his wrists and a large H across his chest—would relieve the pressure of his ballooning body and help save his extremities.

Even though he was unconscious and deeply sedated, Alvaro grimaced at the first cut of the scalpel.

Collette Pritchard, a veteran burn nurse, watched and prayed. *God give him the strength to get through this,* she thought, *whether it is to live or to die.*

Outside, at the nurses' station, the telephones continued to ring incessantly with calls from worried parents wanting to know about their children. The staff couldn't keep up. Even more troubling, some of those who had been waiting in the ER were now gathering outside the burn unit. Information was slow in coming, people were desperate for word, and frustrations were at the boiling point. One woman cried as she pleaded for answers. A distraught father repeatedly shouted his son's name. The staff sympathized, but they couldn't afford to have chaos in the unit. Manzo was young and strapping, and she could be as intimidating with strangers as she was nurturing to her patients. She marched out to the hall but stopped short, shocked at the size of the crowd that had amassed. There were at least a dozen people standing there. A mural of worried, tear-streaked faces stared back at her, some accusingly. *Where the hell is security?* she wondered.

"Look," she said, trying to sound earnest, "I know you're anxious to know about your loved ones, and as soon as we can, we will come out to talk to all of you. Right now we are treating some very sick people and we need you to try to be patient."

A pack of boys, Seton Hall students, walked toward Manzo, threatening to push through the door.

She took a step toward them.

"Stop," she said. "You can't come in. Not even family members are allowed in. Now, pull yourselves together. We're all on the same side here."

"Our friends are in there," one of the students cried. "They need us. There's nobody with them who cares about them."

"I care," Manzo said.

In the midst of the crowd, Daisy Llanos, Alvaro's mother, watched helplessly as Manzo turned to walk back inside. For the two previous nights, Daisy, a superstitious woman, had had a premonition that misfortune was about to visit her only son. It had so unsettled her that to try to comfort herself, she had slept in her son's old bed at home on both nights. When someone from the hospital called to say there had been a fire and Alvaro had been burned, Daisy was overcome with a sense of doom. "How can this be?" she cried. "Alvaro is safe in school. I just saw him two days ago."

Daisy had jumped in the car and driven seventeen miles from Paterson to Saint Barnabas, expecting the worst. A native of Colombia, Daisy spoke very little English, and her husband spoke even less. Her son had always been her voice, her link to the English-speaking world. Now she struggled to be heard. "Permiso, señorita," she said, gently pushing her way to the front of the crowd. *Excuse me, miss.*

"My son is Alvaro Llanos," she said, tears streaming down her cheeks. "Mi hijo es mi vida. ¿Puedes decirme, por favor? ¿Está él vivo?" *My son is my life. Can you tell me, please? Is he alive?*

"Please try to be patient," another nurse said. "The doctor will be out to speak to you as soon as he can."

Chapter 4

With the worst of the burned students finally tucked into their rooms, Mansour was ready to talk to their families. He glanced at his watch. It wasn't yet noon. He had already done a day's work—and then some. He was physically and emotionally drained. In all his years treating burn patients, Mansour had never figured out how to handle his emotions when it came to children. It deeply pained him to see them suffer and always sent him into a profound funk.

Walking out of the burn ICU and down the hall toward the waiting area, he wondered about the two most badly burned boys. The next few hours were critical for their survival. He wasn't sure either would make it through the day. The Simons boy had a fighting chance, but his hands would probably have to be amputated. The Llanos kid would need a miracle to pull through. And if he *did* survive, Mansour wondered, would he be one of those victims who, after all was said and done, was angry that his life had been saved?

The waiting area was jammed with people, crying, praying, glued to a suspended TV set. Mansour glanced up to see what they were watching. CNN was showing footage of the burning dormitory, but the sound was turned off. Mansour didn't blame them. The news coming out of the university was heart wrenching. Three freshman boys were dead: John Giunta, a talented musician, had been trapped in his room and suffocated in the smoke. Two boys—Aaron Karol, a soccer player and scholar from Green Brook, a small township in central New Jersey, and Frank Caltabilota, whose high school football career had made him a hometown hero in Long Branch, a beach city on the Jersey shore—had burned to death in the third-floor lounge. One fire official said he thought Karol and Caltabilota had left their dorm rooms, become disoriented in the smoke, and run into the fire, which was believed to have started in the third-floor lounge.

Caltabilota.

The name sounded familiar to Mansour. *Oh yes,* he realized, *the man who has been calling the burn unit all morning looking for his son.* Each time he had called, someone had checked and double-checked the blackboard by the nurses' station for the names of new patients, and each time they'd had to tell the poor man his son's name was not on it. The man had been increasingly frantic with every call.

Just a boy . . . And now he was gone forever. Mansour shook his head, hoping Mr. Caltabilota hadn't learned of his son's death on the television news.

Dozens of students had suffered burns and smoke inhalation in the fast-moving fire, according to the news reports. Officials didn't know what had caused it yet. One critically burned girl, a resident assistant named Dana Christmas, had been taken to University Hospital in Newark after heroically reentering the burning building several times to alert sleeping students. Most of the seriously injured, the news continued, had landed in the burn unit at Saint Barnabas. The less serious had been treated in the emergency room and released to their parents.

Poignant stories had begun trickling out. One boy had jumped from the ledge outside his third-story window, breaking an arm and a leg. Another heaved a mattress out of his window and was about to jump when a fireman burst into his room and carried him to safety. A girl dialed 911 and was told by a fire dispatcher to stuff a comforter under her door and seal it tight with packing tape. The advice had saved her life. Students told stories of seeing fellow students on fire. One boy had started to flee from the building but found another student—he didn't know his name—lying in a heap just outside his dorm room door. He pulled the gasping student inside, wrapped him in a sweatshirt, and stayed with him until help arrived. A female student, a distance runner on the college track team, nearly tripped over a burned boy as she ran from the fire. She picked him up and carried him outside.

But many of the stories were not as inspiring. Parents spoke of being unable to find their children. One father said he had called his son's cell phone, and his son's roommate had answered. "I can't talk," the boy had exclaimed. "The firemen are trying to get us out." "Where is my son?" the father had asked. "He may have gotten out the back," the roommate said, and cut off the connection. The father still hadn't found his son.

Mansour looked around at the distraught parents, at their eyes, puffy from crying, and their mouths, pinched in grimaces, and his thoughts drifted to his own son. How many nights had he been preoccupied with that most terrible fear of losing your own child? How many prayers had he said, asking that Nicolas never be burned? That was why he had been so insistent that they practice the fire escape route at home, and why he had checked Nicolas's dorm room in Washington for smoke detectors and sprinklers. He would definitely send Nicolas that ladder he and Claudette were talking about.

Shawn Simons and Alvaro Llanos were Nicolas's age. They had the same dreams, the same expectations, the same carefree "nothing can happen to me" attitude that boys their age deserved to have. Mansour shook his head. Now they were in drug-induced comas in the burn center's intensive care section. Respirators were breathing for them. Swaddled in layers of gauze to protect their oozing, burned skin, they looked like mummies. A web of IV lines pumped massive amounts of narcotics and fluids into their bloodstreams to numb them to the unrelenting pain they would otherwise suffer and to prevent deadly burn shock.

What would he tell their parents? That they would sleep that way for weeks? Perhaps months? That is, *if* they lived.

Christine Simons was the first to introduce herself.

Mansour had noticed her, sitting there, comforting the parents of the Llanos boy. He had heard through the hospital grapevine that she had spent most of the morning in the emergency room, making a fuss because the doctors down there had insisted she stay until her blood pressure normalized. She just wanted to be with her son. Mansour didn't blame her; he admired her mettle.

"What can you tell us, Doctor?" Christine asked when she saw Mansour standing there.

"The next few months will be a roller-coaster ride," Mansour replied. If their boys did survive, they would lose months and maybe even years of their lives to the healing process, and even then their scars—both physical and emotional—might be permanent.

Alvaro's sister Shirley translated the doctor's words into Spanish for her parents. In any language they were unwelcome, and Daisy Llanos wiped away tears.

Her son. Tall. Handsome. Her golden boy. He had willingly taken on the role of head of the family after her husband's stroke two years earlier. He truly was the perfect child, and now she might lose him.

"I want to know why I thought my son was sleeping in the dormitory, safe. Why someone wakes me up to tell me he's in the hospital," she cried. Mansour didn't have an answer. He couldn't say why the fire had happened, and he couldn't say whether her son would survive.

Alvaro senior leaned heavily on his cane for support.

"Is my son afraid?" he asked.

"No," Mansour said. "He is sleeping, probably dreaming." He paused for just a moment. "We hope," Hani said, "they are good dreams."

Chapter 5

Mansour had been at the hospital all day and half the night when he finally pulled on his overcoat and switched off the desk lamp in his windowless office. All he wanted was a shower and some sleep.

It was already past ten o'clock and he had been on his feet for sixteen hours. He was due back in the burn unit at 7 A.M. He hoped the two most badly injured boys were still alive when he returned, but he had learned long ago just how cunning burns could be. Keeping a professional distance was the only way to stay sane. How many times had he seen hope turn to despair with the tick of the second hand on a clock? More times than he liked to admit. Such was the business of burns. Recovery was erratic, fraught with fleeting highs and long, dreadful lows.

Walking down the hall through the burn ICU, Mansour passed room 4, where Alvaro Llanos lay motionless, his parents at his bedside. Mansour stopped and peered through the glass. The boy was covered with gauze from his head to his feet; only his toes poked through his suit of hospital armor. His arms, tied above his head to keep him from unconsciously yanking out his respirator hose, made him look like a ghoulish contortionist in the middle of a trick.

Mansour hadn't been able to say what the prognosis was for Shawn or for Alvaro, although the parents of both boys had asked the question over and over again that day. The truth was that either one of them could die at any time. Indeed, they were living on stolen moments. When the boys did wake up, they would most likely not remember the fire or the initial pain of their burns, Mansour had said.

"But they will survive," Christine had said, making a statement, not asking a question.

"At this point, we just can't say," Mansour had replied. "This is a very delicate time. Right now, we just don't know."

Alvaro's condition was particularly precarious. Mansour was fairly certain that if Shawn survived, he would lose all of his fingers. But Alvaro would lose his identity. Neither he nor his life would resemble what it had been before the fire. How much he made of his life as a burned person would depend on his character, but that question was a long way off.

"Pray," had been the only answer Mansour was able to give the boy's parents, earlier that day, when they asked what they could do to help their son. Now Hani watched as Alvaro's mother and father stood over their unconscious son, praying in Spanish.

The Llanoses were loving parents. Mansour could see that. But he had found them hard to reach when he spoke to them earlier that day. He wasn't sure if their expressions were dazed because they understood so little English, or because they were just so bewildered by what was happening. He was certain they did not comprehend that their son's situation was perilous, or that if he survived, he would be in a coma for a very long time.

Deep in prayer, neither parent noticed Mansour watching the scene.

He walked on.

The families had a long road ahead of them. In some ways, their journey would be more difficult than their children's.

For the parents, there was little to do but wait and worry. Mansour knew how agonizing it was for them. He wished there was a magic pill to help ease their suffering. For now, he had done all he could for their children.

Christine and Kenny Simons were watching television in the waiting room. They had asked if they could bunk there to be close to Shawn.

"Good night, folks," Mansour said, stopping at the door.

"How is Shawn, Doctor?" Christine asked.

"Sleeping tight," Mansour said, trying to offer some comfort. "Now get some rest. Tomorrow will be another long day."

Mansour had liked the Simonses right away. Both seemed bright and levelheaded. From what he had been able to glean so far, he guessed they were stronger than Daisy and Alvaro Llanos, who were disadvantaged by the language barrier and the effects of Alvaro senior's stroke. Christine Simons had already won over the nurses with her easy smile and warm way. They marveled at her composure under such terrible pressure. She had even taken the Llanoses under her wing and seemed to be able to comfort them, although she didn't speak a word of Spanish. And her devotion to her son was palpable, pure, and beautiful.

If the boys lived, they would be in the burn unit for a long, long time. Family support would mean as much as a dose of good luck. Hani could already see that Alvaro's case was one that the nurses would debate late at night during breaks in the cafeteria: Were they doing him a disservice by trying to save him? Mansour wasn't sure Alvaro's parents were up to the task they faced. There were times when he himself looked at patients he had treated and thought, *My God, what have I done?* As he walked out of Saint Barnabas and back to his Jeep for the ride home, he prayed this would not be one of them.

Chapter 6

Hani Mansour had heard his first burn scream when he was just a boy, growing up in Beirut, Lebanon, in the 1950s. The sound was unlike anything he had ever known. It seemed to start deep in the gut, then build slowly, deliberately, until it finally spilled out into a long, tortured wail.

Hani wasn't yet a teenager. He was visiting his ailing father in Beirut's military hospital when he heard the person in the next room screaming in pain.

"What is the matter with that man?" young Hani asked a nurse on duty that day.

"The man was burned in a house fire," the nurse replied.

"Why can't you help him?" Hani asked.

"There is nothing to do but wait for him to die," the nurse said resignedly.

For days afterward, young Hani could hear the scream in his sleep. And whenever the wail replayed in his mind, the boy would squeeze his eyes shut and shake his head—hoping to rattle the memory right out of his brain.

It was twenty years later, as a young doctor beginning his career in Lebanon's largest city, that Mansour heard the unmistakable scream again. He was working as a resident in general surgery at Saint George Greek Orthodox Hospital in Beirut. A senior physician had assigned him to care for a group of soldiers burned by napalm during the 1973 Arab-Israeli War. The plastic surgeon on staff didn't want to deal with the soldiers, and Mansour was put in charge of their treatment. The memory of the man from his childhood still haunted him and he felt a sense of responsibility to do all he could to ease the soldiers' suffering.

Lebanon was just gaining its independence from France when Esber "Hani" Mansour was born in July 1947. Beirut, a Mediterranean seaside metropolis, was crowned the new capital city. Mansour's father, Nicolas, owned a construction company and built apartment buildings there. His mother, Marie, was the daughter of a physician. The Mansour family was by no means wealthy, but they were educated and members of Beirut's intellectual class. That was saying something, because Beirut was considered the intellectual capital of the Middle East.

Marie Mansour had always hoped one of her five sons would follow in the footsteps of her altruistic father and study to become a doctor. But her husband had other ideas, and four of the boys followed him into engineering. That left Hani, the middle son, and his mother pushed him hard toward a career in medicine. Following her wishes, he applied to and was accepted at both American University and Saint Joseph's University in Beirut. He chose Saint Joseph's, but his mother's dreams almost ended on the first day of classes. A microbiology professor was lecturing about "echinococcus that multiply by schizogony," and he might as well have been speaking a foreign language. Hani suddenly realized he was in way over his head. He went home and told his mother he wasn't going back. She, however, had other ideas. And Hani returned. In the end, he knew he couldn't let her down.

For the longest time after earning his medical degree, Mansour couldn't decide on a specialty. Perhaps if the dream had been his own and not his mother's, he would have been more focused. It took the severely burned soldiers to stir his passion. If no one else cared enough to try to get past the grisliness and the hopelessness of their condition, then he was determined to help them in whatever way he could.

Back then, in Beirut, burn treatment was undeveloped, and practitioners were scarcer than scarce, so Mansour turned to textbooks for guidance. The history was fascinating. In 1500 B.C. the Egyptians had used mud and cow dung to treat burns. Things hadn't gotten much better by the seventh century, when a salve concocted of "old wild hogs and bears and a chunk of genuine mummy" was recommended, or the seventeenth century, when turpentine and maggots were the preferred option. Only after World War I and the terrible toll that modern warfare had taken on the human race was the medical profession forced to pay closer attention to burns, and only then did physicians even begin to realize how little they knew about treating them. World War II brought advances in anesthesia, skin-grafting techniques, and the use of penicillin to treat infection, a deadly side effect of burns. Back on the home front, the 1942 Cocoanut Grove nightclub fire in Boston, which killed 492 people and injured hundreds more, started a revolution in burn treatment research. Using the surviving patients as guinea pigs, doctors in Massachusetts not only treated the surface burns but also focused for the first time on the internal effects of burn injuries. By treating respiratory injuries and shock as well as burns, doctors saved more patients from the Cocoanut Grove and every fire since than would otherwise have survived.

By the 1960s, doctors were infusing burn patients with liquid formulas to replace the huge amounts of plasma leaking through their pores. Later advances in topical antibiotics to fight septicemia, a massive infection from burns that poisons the blood, further reduced the death rate.

Still, the prognosis for the burned soldiers in the 1970s wasn't much better than it had been for the poor man Mansour had encountered twenty years earlier while visiting his father in the hospital. It still held true, after all those years and all of the experimental treatments, that major burns, like the ones caused by napalm, were almost always fatal, and the rare patient who did survive often succumbed to the relentless infections.

Doctors were healers, so few of them wanted to take up a specialty where the outlook for patients was so often grim. Mansour started to see it differently. Most doctors looked at a burn patient and saw hopelessness; he saw a field that desperately needed developing and that appealed to the sense of ingenuity he had inherited from his engineer father. Looking at the Syrian soldiers, Hani Mansour saw his future.

Once Mansour had his specialty, he threw himself into it, researching the latest treatments and spending hours at the bedsides of his patients, trying to soothe the excruciating pain of their burns and ease their fears of dying—or worse, living. Mansour spent a year practicing at the Beirut hospital. At the time, civil unrest was simmering in Lebanon. Tensions between Christians and Muslims were bubbling up, and the Lebanese Civil War would soon tear the capital city apart. Before long, Beirut would be divided by religion, with Muslims living in the west and Christians in the east. Many of the residents would flee to other countries rather than carry on amid the growing turmoil. Mansour, a Catholic, decided to further his medical career by studying in America, where the postgraduate training was a decade ahead of Lebanon's program.

In December 1974, Mansour immigrated to the United States and began his residency in general surgery at Union Memorial Medical Center in Baltimore. The only thing Baltimore and Beirut had in common was the *B*, and Hani longed for his homeland and his family. The only compensation was the residency itself. Mansour was constantly stimulated, learning new treatment methods that encouraged him to reconceive what might be possible with regard to the severely burned.

Six months after he got to the United States, Mansour was introduced to an erudite American nurse named Claudette Crochetiere. Claudette had just returned from six months in France, where she had worked as an au pair in a *pension de famille* (boarding house) in Paris to be able to live among the French and learn their language. In Baltimore, she was studying for a master's degree in public health at Johns Hopkins University and working nights as a nurse in a surgery ward at Union Memorial. When she heard the new resident speaking fluent French on the telephone, she struck up a conversation. Hani invited Claudette out for pizza that night. After a three-year courtship, he proposed, and they married in a small ceremony at Claudette's parents' home in Connecticut in 1978.

They hadn't been married a year when Mansour applied for a fellowship to study under the preeminent burn surgeon Basil Pruitt at the U.S. Army Institute of Surgical Research at Fort Sam Houston in San Antonio, Texas. From everything Mansour had heard, Texas was a dusty, sticky place where men wore cowboy hats and carried guns in their trucks. He didn't care. The base was touted as the army's premier medical training center, and Pruitt's burn unit was considered the best in the world. Mansour was accepted into Pruitt's program, but because he was a civilian, not a soldier, he was told he would only be allowed to observe. No, no, Mansour said. He wanted hands-on training. The only way would be to join the army, Pruitt said. The timing was certainly right. Army doctors were in short supply when the draft was abolished near the end of the Vietnam War, and Mansour was a willing recruit. By agreeing to serve two years, he was able to join even though he was not a citizen.

With his new orders in hand, Hani and Claudette packed up their matching Chevy Vegas and drove seventeen hundred miles from Baltimore to San Antonio during a gas shortage. From the Middle East to the Lone Star State within five years—life certainly took some strange twists and turns, he thought.

It was the first time in Claudette's life that she had started over for someone else. Having grown up in a close-knit family from Connecticut, she was used to being around her brothers and sisters. With no job, no friends, and no family close by, she was instantly lonely, but Hani was single minded: he was going to be a burn surgeon. In San Antonio, Hani and Claudette took out a VA loan and put five hundred dollars down on a house near the army base. Within months, Claudette was pregnant with their son, Nicolas.

In short order, Pruitt promoted his younger protégé to chief of burn study, and Mansour's career was sealed. At the same time, burn treatment was in the midst of a second minirevolution. Since the discovery of penicillin and what was learned from the Cocoanut Grove fire, there had been few new remedies or treatments. But in the 1970s, topical antibiotics came into wide use. The medical profession also began to understand how to use nutrition to prevent a burn patient's body, which was in a hypermetabolic state, from consuming itself. The technique of skin grafting using cultured and artificial skin was on the horizon. Survival rates had doubled since Mansour's college years in Beirut, and the number of burn centers in the United States had tripled in the preceding decade, to more than one hundred.

Mansour had been in San Antonio only a few months when, on October 19, 1979, Typhoon Tip roared into mainland Japan. The storm packed 115-mile-per-hour winds and torrential rain. More than 1,250 U.S. Marines were housed in Quonset huts at a base known as Camp Fuji. The camp's fuel farm was up the hill from the huts. The downpour eroded the retaining walls around the fuel storage bladders, and one broke free, spilling five thousand gallons of gasoline into the huts. A space heater sparked the fuel, and the huts ruptured into flames, killing thirteen marines. The seventy-two burn victims were airlifted to Pruitt's burn center in San Antonio. The worst was burned over 92 percent of his body. Ten years earlier, he would surely have died, but Mansour was able to save his life using the newest treatments.

Two years later, Saint Barnabas contacted Pruitt, looking for a recommendation for someone to head up its budding burn unit. Pruitt didn't even need to think about it. Mansour was thirty-four at the time and had learned enough to pursue his dream of returning to Lebanon to open a burn unit there. But the civil war raged on. The opportunity to work in the New York area with some of the brightest minds in medicine was too good to pass up, and he agreed to postpone his dream of going home. He would go to New Jersey—but only for a year.

In Texas, he and Claudette lived fifteen miles and one traffic light from the hospital, and even that distance he thought was too far. So when they came to New Jersey to look for a place to live, Hani bought a map and drew a five-mile circle around Saint Barnabas. Whatever house they bought would have to be somewhere in that ring, he told the real estate agent. The first house he set his sights on was directly across the street from the hospital, so close that at night the lights in the hospital parking lot lit up the living room. Claudette, who had a toddler to care for, put her foot down. They settled on a home two miles away.

Mansour arrived at Saint Barnabas in the summer of 1981 and found a ten-bed burn center tucked in a corner of the hospital basement. The beds were half empty and the small staff were green. He hired more staff and taught nurses, technicians, even plastic surgeons, how to treat burns. The burn unit grew as doctors and nurses were drawn to this modern hospital in northern New Jersey by the possibility of working with Hani. One year turned to ten, and his dream of returning to Lebanon sat on the shelf, collecting dust.

Mansour was known as impish and eccentric. Some days he arrived at work wearing one black shoe and one brown. He tended to exasperate his staff with his demands and his absentmindedness, but their admiration was boundless and uld do anything to accommodate him. When he ded someone to work a double shift or an overnight shift, five people would volunteer. He was the kind of doctor they could have fun with, too. When he was dieting, the nurses hid the birthday cakes from him. He could be moody and quick to anger, pouting when he gained a pound and blowing up when someone suggested that a homeless man who had deliberately set himself on fire deserved less consideration than a burn patient who was less culpable. When children were admitted to the unit, he could be glum for days. Yet whenever the stress in the unit grew nearly unbearable, it was Mansour who broke it by telling one of his corny jokes, then laughing the hardest of all. When he laughed, his whole body jiggled and his face turned scarlet.

Under Mansour, the burn unit had moved up from the windowless corner in the basement to a sunny wing on the second floor to accommodate the ever-growing staff of ninety, including surgeons, nurses, social workers, and respiratory, physical, and occupational therapists. A unit that had had only ten beds when he took over now had thirty. Before Mansour knew it, nineteen years had gone by. The Saint Barnabas Burn Center was recognized as one of the top burn treatment centers on the East Coast. The gruesome nature of the work meant that few ever became old-timers in the occupation of treating burns. Those who did were the best in the business. And those few were found at Saint Barnabas, hiding sweets from their boss.

Chapter 7

At three in the morning, there wasn't much to do in a hospital waiting room, and Kenny Simons had that leg-jittering kind of restlessness. A television was on, but the sound was turned off. Fluorescent bulbs on the ceiling lit up the tiny space like Hollywood spotlights, flooding the room with an intense and antiseptic atmosphere.

Kenny was sitting in a wooden chair so hard it didn't move even as his leg jackhammered into the floor. Nearby, Christine lay curled up on a couch with her eyes closed. Watching the minutes tick by on a large, round wall clock, he tried not to think about the time. Or the lights. Or facing the world with a mangled son. He had always been so proud of his handsome boy. He loved the way his skin had been as smooth as a baby's, even though he was in college now. *How will Shawn handle being disfigured? How will he handle people staring? How will I?* Kenny wondered, the cacophony of thoughts getting louder in his head.

"I'm worried about how Shawn is going to handle how he looks," he announced, hoping his ex-wife wasn't really asleep.

Of course, Christine wasn't sleeping. She hadn't slept a wink in the two days since Shawn had been burned. How do you sleep when your child is fighting for his life? How do you sleep when your ex-husband is squirming and fidgeting less than an arm's length away? Sometimes, Christine wondered why Kenny was even there. He had hardly been a doting father since he'd left them, at her insistence, fourteen years earlier. She hadn't forgotten the times he'd missed Shawn's birthday or the Christmas when he neglected to give him a single gift. Shawn had never been more hurt than he'd been when Kenny had told him, years earlier, "I have a new family now. You'll have to accept your place in the background."

Christine sat up on the couch and pulled the blanket around her shoulders. "What are you talking about, Kenny?" she asked.

"When I was young, I was handsome like him," he said. "If he's anything like me, he's going to be devastated by this."

Anything like you? Anything like you? Shawn is sweet and kind. He's considerate of me and his sister. He thinks about other people, not just himself. Shawn isn't anything like you.

Christine bit her tongue so her thoughts couldn't spill out into words. She had always tried to be polite to Kenny. She had never pursued him for any kind of monetary support, and when he had made appearances in Shawn's life over the years, she had always been gracious. But this was too much.

Shawn was lying in a bed in a burn unit, hovering somewhere between life and death. There was a real chance he would never look back at her, never tell her another funny story, never giggle at one of her silly jokes, never throw his arms around her and say, *Mom, how did I get so lucky to have you as my mother?*

Tears welled up in Christine's eyes. She didn't hear what Kenny was saying anymore, but he was saying something and she cut him off.

"We're waiting to see if God is going to spare our child, and you're thinking about Shawn's *looks?* What's the matter with you, Kenny? Instead of sitting here crying about the way he might look, you should be on your knees praying that he's still with us in the morning."

It was the last night they would spend together in the hospital.

The team of seven arson investigators had scoured every inch of Boland Hall, looking for clues about how the fire started. Working under bright klieg lights, they formed an assembly line and shoveled debris into neat piles. Then they sifted through every inch of ash and gunk for evidence. When they walked out of Boland Hall after midnight, they had eliminated most of the typical causes of accidental fires. They had checked every electrical socket and wire. They had searched for space heaters and found none. "We believe the area of origin was the couch beneath the bulletin board in the third-floor lounge," Frucci wrote in his report.

The early investigation revealed that the fire had been searing and quick, a twelve- to fifteen-minute event that probably started with an "open ignition"—a match or a lighter. There was no evidence of accelerants.

The team suspected arson, but they couldn't prove it. Their only hope was to find someone who had seen something suspicious.

Within twenty-four hours of the blaze, investigators had begun interviewing students. They learned that Boland Hall had been a rowdy place on the night of the fire. There had been parties after the basketball game, and kids were drunk and rambunctious. Boys had been wrestling in the third-floor lounge. The resident advisers had tried to calm them, but it had done no good.

Two students offered a curious observation. From their dorm room, they said, they had heard the sound of paper being torn down, like a banner being ripped off the wall. Then everything had gone silent—until the fire alarms began wailing.

That was helpful information, but the cause remained a mystery. Maybe the banner was deliberately torn down, or maybe it just came down on its own when the tape adhering it to the wall lost its stick. Maybe the two students were wrong about what they had heard. And even if they were right, what did that prove? Frucci was stuck.

Little did he know that he was about to get his first break.

It was Sunday. Investigators had interviewed dozens of students in the four days since the fire and they were frustrated at how little they still knew.

Sean Ryan was one of several students at the South Orange police headquarters that afternoon, a random name on a list of some two hundred Boland Hall residents who still needed to be questioned.

Seated on the other side of a metal desk from his state police interrogator, Sgt. Kevin Dunn, a ruddy-faced Irishman with a crew cut, the boy had seemed calm enough at first.

Yes, Ryan said, he lived in Boland Hall.

Yes, he had been horsing around in the dorm with friends after the basketball game.

No, he didn't know anything about the fire.

Cops walked in and out of the tiny interrogation room. One hour turned to two, then three. Ryan fidgeted in his chair. He was tired and feeling the pressure. Suddenly, he turned weepy.

The worst thing he had done that night was pull a paper banner off the wall in the lounge, he finally admitted. He certainly hadn't started any fire. No way.

Frucci watched from his seat in the corner. The air seemed to leave the room. No one breathed as Dunn exchanged a quick look with Frucci. Frucci read his expression as saying *Holy shit.*

Frucci and Dunn were thinking the same thing: two students had said they heard the sound of paper being torn down in the third-floor lounge right before the fire alarm rang. The banner was hanging over the same couch in the lounge that arson investigators had determined was where the fire began.

State Police lieutenant Christopher Andreychak was the next to speak.

So, hypothetically, if you knew who lit the fire, would you tell us? Andreychak asked Ryan nonchalantly.

The boy turned cold. "Well, I'm no rat," he said.

It was a strange answer, Frucci thought, and a telling one.

Dunn turned to his computer and perched his fingers over the keyboard. It was time to take Ryan's official statement.

Ryan stared at his interrogators. He had said too much and he seemed to know it. He rose from his chair to leave. There would be no formal statement, Ryan said. Not today.

"I'll be back tomorrow," he said, walking toward the door.

Would he take a polygraph then? Dunn asked.

Yeah, sure, Ryan promised, fleeing the room.

Dunn looked at Frucci and Andreychak. "That kid's never coming back," he said. And that, they thought, was interesting—maybe more than interesting.

There were a couple of reasons why Sean Ryan would not be back to take a polygraph. For one, two days earlier, at a meeting at the local Dunkin' Donuts, he had made a pact with Joey LePore, his Boland Hall roommate, to say nothing to police about the night of the fire. Ryan and LePore had been best friends since kindergarten, and like all best friends, they had shared plenty of secrets.

Their biggest secret was the second reason Ryan would not be back.

Chapter 8

The tank room was the heart of burn treatment. Antiseptic, windowless, and brightly lit with fluorescent lights, it looked like other hospital treatment rooms—except that it wasn't. It was foul smelling and muggy. Between the heat and the sickening odors of burned flesh and open wounds, medical students were known to faint fairly frequently.

The tank room was what burn patients tended to remember most about their hospital stay—even years later. It was the place where they were taken every day to have their open wounds scrubbed with gauze that felt more like sandpaper or Brillo. Called debridement, the scouring was a fundamental step in burn treatment. Proteins leaked from the wounds and formed a film that looked like the cooked white of an egg. The film, which provided a haven for deadly infections, dried into a hard, waxy scab. When it was scrubbed away early in the treatment process, permanent scarring was minimized and the risk of infections was limited.

Most patients were heavily sedated in the burn unit, but they were injected with booster shots of morphine before they were delivered for their tank treatment. They still felt the pain.

Paul Mellini, the chief tank-room technician, had scheduled Alvaro early. His tank time was exhausting for the staff, both physically and emotionally, and they wanted to get through it as quickly as possible. A tanking usually took an hour or less; Alvaro's took two hours every time. "Let's go," Mellini said as four others followed him into room 4, where the comatose boy lay. Two doors away a two-month-old baby, purposely scalded by his mother in a bathtub and admitted the night before, was screaming. An elderly woman burned in a cooking accident moaned in the room beyond that.

The mood in Alvaro's room was tense. At five feet ten inches tall and two hundred pounds, Alvaro Llanos was not a small man. With seventy extra pounds of fluids in his body, and grisly, gaping sores branding his torso, he looked more like a decaying corpse than a living human being.

Alvaro was the largest patient in the burn unit, and the sickest. Unconscious, he was dead weight and difficult to handle. The team of nurses and technicians who arrived in his room to take him for his daily scouring in the tank room had had to gear themselves up for it.

On the count of three, Mellini and his team lifted Alvaro off his bed and onto a plastic-covered, stainless-steel shower trolley. They covered him with a blanket and then rolled the trolley twenty-five feet into the tank room and under a trio of shower hoses that hung from the ceiling. The trolley was tipped slightly and another hose was attached from the bottom of the gurney to a drain in the floor. That hose would accommodate the runoff of water, blood, and dead flesh. Mellini tried to keep the atmosphere light. "Save me a piece of birthday cake from the lunchroom," he said to one of the burn technicians as he raised a pair of shiny silver scissors and began cutting away the bloodstained gauze from Alvaro's arm.

"Livin' La Vida Loca" played on a boom box in the room. "Living the crazy life, that's us," Alvaro's nurse, Andy Horvath, declared. Everyone nervously laughed at his comment.

The team cut away the gauze covering every inch of Alvaro's body except his feet, his eyes, his nostrils, and his lips. Horvath pumped additional morphine into an IV line in Alvaro's arm as they stripped away the bandages. Soon Alvaro was naked. The room went quiet. From his scalp to his waist, Alvaro was one gaping, oozing wound. His hands, grafted earlier, were a brownish purple, bloated to twice their normal size. His hair had been burned off and his head was red and shiny, and chunks of his ears were missing. The sides of his torso were concave, the burns so deep that the surgeons had been forced to cut away layers of flesh to reach healthy tissue to support the temporary, life-sustaining skin grafts he had received when he was first brought into the hospital. But his back was the worst: a skinless bed of raw red and yellow tissue. Even his legs, which were not burned, had not been spared. So much healthy skin had been taken from his legs to graft onto his torso and his back that they now looked like a patchwork quilt.

Horvath choked up.

"Let's get to work," Mellini said.

They soaked Alvaro with warm tap water from the overhead hoses. Then they smeared him with antibacterial soap and began scrubbing his burns with four-by-four-inch gauze pads, the ones patients said felt like steel wool.

While the team scrubbed, Mellini watched Alvaro's face to gauge how much pain they were causing him. Though out cold, Alvaro grimaced. Then, despite being in a morphine-induced state of unconsciousness, he lifted his right arm as if to ward off the next punch. Nelly Delgado, a grandmother who had worked in the tank room longer than anyone else, was overcome by tears. Alvaro was hooked to a respirator and unable to make sounds, but she knew he was screaming inside. "Okay, honey," Delgado said, tears rolling out of her eyes. "I'm so sorry I'm hurting you. Poor baby. God help our poor, poor baby."

Horvath, a gentle man, beloved by the patients and the rest of the staff, stroked Alvaro's bare hands. He had already become attached to the boy. He had seen the pictures the Llanoses taped to the wall near their son's bed: Alvaro holding his girlfriend, Angie Gutierrez; posing with his parents and sisters in their kitchen; mugging for the camera with his buddies from Paterson. The photographs showed a beautiful boy with soft, romantic eyes and a cocky smile. Horvath had instantly become fiercely protective of him.

"I'll take care of his face," he told the others.

"Okay, Al," Horvath said quietly as he began his work. "It's okay. You're doing fine, buddy. I'm going to clean your mouth now. Good boy. Oh, you have the most beautiful white teeth."

With the cleaning finished, Alvaro was moved to the other side of the curtain that divided the tank room. There, he was placed under a heat shield to keep him warm. Toni Schmidt, a burn technician, picked up a silver nitrate stick. It looked as harmless as a Q-tip. She touched the end of the stick to one of the open wounds on Alvaro's right side to oxidize unwanted scar tissue. To Alvaro, it would feel as if he were being burned all over again. How intense was the pain that, even unconscious, the boy seemed to feel it? Beyond imagining. Tears streamed from Alvaro's eyes. Nearby, a table had been prepared with his new dressings—large pieces of gauze slathered with brownish yellow silver sulfadiazine, a topical antimicrobial cream. The team wrapped the gauze around Alvaro from his head to his ankles, rolled him onto a stretcher, covered him with a blanket, and, at 9:55 A.M., pushed him back to his room.

The procedure had taken one hour and fifty-five minutes. Tomorrow morning it would begin all over again.

Chapter 9

The ambulance, sirens blaring, rolled up to the gilded gates outside Seton Hall, and Shawn could hardly believe what he saw.

There must have been a thousand people waiting, and they were chanting his name. *Shawn . . . Shawn . . . Shawn.*

The ambulance stopped and he quickly slid out from the passenger seat. The crowd roared. As soon as his feet hit the grass, a marching band struck up a rendition of "When the Saints Go Marching In." It was one of his favorite tunes. Shawn felt like the king of a pageant. It was good to be back, he thought, surveying the lush, green campus.

There was Monsignor Robert Sheeran, wearing a huge grin. And the Seton Hall cheerleaders, dressed in the school colors, blue and white, turned cartwheels as they shouted out the letters of his name.

S-H-A-W-N. *What does it spell?*

SHAWN! the crowd screamed.

Boland Hall sat majestically at the top of a grassy knoll. Like the Pied Piper, Shawn led the throng to the front of the building.

There sat a brand-new red Mustang with gleaming silver wheels. It was the most beautiful car he had ever seen, and it was for him.

Shawn felt warm from the inside out.

Only it was all a morphine dream.

The familiar rhythm of the respirator had come to be a comfort to Christine. There was something peculiarly soothing about it, predictable—a sound she could count on to fill the terrible silence.

For fourteen days and nights, Christine had sat at Shawn's bedside, looking for a sign that he was still there, under all the tubes and wires and whirring machines. A twitch, a sniff, anything would do. Sometimes she thought she saw him blink, but then she realized her eyes were deceiving her. If only she knew what he was thinking now. Was he afraid? Did he know what was happening to him? Was he hurting?

The truth was, she was suffering along with Shawn. Sometimes she stared at his face until her back ached, hoping for a sign. Her sweet son—the boy who put the joy in her life—lay there in a continuous sleep, a web of IV lines pushing food, liquids, and narcotics into his bloodstream. His eyes were swollen shut and his arms were tied to the bed so that he didn't unconsciously try to pull out his breathing tube. Day after day, she had nothing to do but watch—and fret about what to do if nothing ever changed.

Shawn had already survived one fire in his young life. He was a month old when their place in Newark burned to the ground. A fire had begun on a stove in the apartment below theirs. Christine had taken Nicole to school and arrived home just in time to see Kenny fleeing from the burning building with their Shawn cradled in his arms. Now she prayed that Shawn's luck hadn't run out.

Every time her mind wandered to such dark places—*What if he never wakes up? What if I never hear his silvery voice? What if I never get to tell him I love him again?*—Christine listened for the whisper of his breathing machine. As the respirator pumped life into her son's oxygen-starved lungs, it soothed her nerves and washed her mind of all thoughts. For a moment, at least.

Shawn felt as if he were being flung around in a plane as it crashed into the ocean. His face stung from spraying water. Then the blast abruptly stopped.

He opened his eyes to a blurry world. All Shawn could make out were the vague forms of strangers, pushing and pulling at him. Someone shouted, "Breathe! Breathe!"

Shawn was in the tank room, and he was awake, three

weeks and one day since the fire. Even the staff were surprised when he suddenly awoke from his coma. There, as they had been cleaning him, Shawn had raised himself up, trying to climb out of his fog. Now he opened his arms and someone embraced him. He heard people crying and applauding. He didn't hear his mother. He wished she were there.

Christine and Kenny had arrived in the burn unit two hours later. Andy Horvath intercepted them as they headed for Shawn's room.

"Hey, Andy," Christine said.

"Shawn's awake," Horvath announced. "He woke up in the tank room."

Christine steadied herself.

"Oh my God," she said.

"He's alert but he's bewildered," Horvath said. "He can't talk because of the respirator, but he wants to communicate."

Christine had been critical of Kenny and his concerns, but while her ex-husband might have been clumsy in conversation and negligent as a parent, underneath it all was a heartfelt recognition of the stakes. Kenny had lost two of his children from his first marriage, and he had prayed every day that God save his son.

"My prayers have been answered," he cried.

Shawn's eyes widened when his mother walked into the room. She knew what he was telling her: *I'm so glad you're here.*

"Baby boy, I have been waiting weeks for this moment," Christine said, tears flooding her eyes.

As relieved as she was, she felt helpless. Mothers were supposed to make their children feel better. She had always been able to do that. But now she saw such pain and fear in Shawn's eyes, and there was nothing she could do except trust in God and the doctors.

Tears trickled down Shawn's badly burned cheeks as he looked from his mother to his father. He tried to speak but couldn't.

"The respirator," Kenny explained. "You won't be able to talk until you're taken off it."

Shawn blinked his eyes hard.

"Your glasses," Christine said. "You can't see very well, can you?"

She took the wire-rimmed glasses from the table beside Shawn's bed and placed them on his face.

He wiggled his bandaged hands.

"As long as you can move them, that's good," his father said.

He raised his hand to his head. His curls. Where were they? "It's okay," Christine reassured him. "They'll come back."

Shawn looked pleadingly into her eyes. He seemed desperate to say something.

Horvath left the room and returned a moment later carrying a large sheet of paper with the alphabet printed on it. Shawn's eyes brightened.

Christine placed the paper in front of Shawn, and slowly but deliberately, he pointed out letters.

W-h-e-r-e h-a-v-e y-o-u b-e-e-n?

"Right here, every day," Christine replied.

Shawn had another question.

H-o-w i-s A-l?

Chapter 10

Daisy Llanos was a devout woman. She spent hours reading the Bible and praying over her son, and she had decorated his hospital room with rainbow-colored rosary beads. When she wasn't in the burn unit, she was at the altar in Saint Joseph's Roman Catholic Church near her home in Paterson. "Please, Jesus, if you love me and you love my son and you love my family, please help us through this," she prayed in Spanish. "Please leave my son with me, no matter how burned he is."

Daisy's prayers had been answered two years earlier when she begged for her husband to survive his life-threatening stroke. She needed another favor now. Alvaro's injuries were grave. His body was mutilated and he was barely alive. He would suffocate if oxygen weren't being continually pumped into his lungs. His eyelids were sewn shut to protect the soft tissue of his burned corneas from hardening. If God let her son live, she would take care of him the way she had taken care of her husband. She would give up everything to help him get better.

Mi niño bello, nadie jamás te hará daño. My beautiful boy, no one will ever hurt you again. She would make sure of it.

As Alvaro waged his lonely fight to stay alive, friends and family members confessed their fears and frustrations in letters that were tacked to his hospital room wall. "Waiting for your response to our presence, but not a single movement has occurred," his sixteen-year-old sister Shany wrote. "Out of everyone in the family, you are the last person we expect to give up . . . I know that when we are in the room with you, you can hear us and I know you're trying to respond." Angie wasn't so sure. "When I lie down I try to hug myself so I can feel your body close to mine," she wrote. "But somehow no matter what I do I can't find you. No matter how hard I try I can't see you."

It was Angie who delivered the news to the Llanoses that Shawn was awake. Daisy tried to be happy. Privately she wondered why it couldn't have been Alvaro who was getting better, and then she prayed to be forgiven for her selfish thoughts.

The Simonses and the Llanoses had bonded in the weeks since the fire. Except for vigils at their sons' bedsides, the families had spent every day together in the burn unit waiting room. They watched *Jerry Springer, Divorce Court,* and *Oprah Winfrey.* They shared trays of fried chicken and macaroni and cheese brought in by a local church. And they talked endlessly about their sons, somehow managing to surmount the language barrier to share their stories. Their boys had been burned together as they crawled their way through the fire and the smoke at Boland Hall, and the families believed they would heal together as well.

Angie had dropped some of her classes to be with Alvaro. When she wasn't sitting beside her comatose boyfriend, saying, "Keep fighting, baby," to encourage him, or chattering about what she had done in school that day, she sat beside Daisy, patting her back or holding her hand. Angie was brave, but Christine was everyone's rock. What she hadn't been able to tell Shawn when he asked about his roommate was that the doctors had given Alvaro only a 40 percent chance of surviving.

On the same day that Shawn woke up, signaling the beginning of his recovery, the nurses in the burn unit debated whether it would be better if Alvaro died. They were sitting around a table in the break room, sharing a pizza for dinner, when the subject came up.

"Al—he gets to you," one of the nurses said. "Have you seen his pictures?" She was referring to the photographs Alvaro's family had taped to the wall in his room. "He was so handsome, a gorgeous kid."

"His father told me he wanted to be a professional baseball player and he was really good," another said.

"His mother keeps asking, 'Will he look the same? Have you seen other people this bad?' I tell her Alvaro is very, very sick. It's day to day. Hour to hour. The next day she asks the same questions all over again."

"From what I know about him, I don't think he'll be able to adjust," said Laura Thompson, a nurse who had worked in the burn unit for fifteen years.

"I'm afraid his parents are too fragile to cope with what's ahead," said Andy Horvath. "I can't even look at them anymore," he added. "They keep asking me when he'll wake up, and I don't want to give them false hope."

Shawn had turned the corner. His life was no longer in danger. Now it was a matter of healing, which could take months. But if Alvaro lived, he would be defined by his burns for the rest of his life. It's time to start separating the families, Chris Ruhren, the director of the burn unit nurses, told the staff. "This can no longer be treated like one case."

Chapter 11

The burn nurses had quickly become attached to Shawn and Alvaro. They celebrated Shawn's victories and they agonized over Alvaro's setbacks. "You're all angels," Christine Simons would say at least once a day to the nurses. One former patient had lapel buttons made up for the staff that read, "There is a special place in heaven saved for those who treat burns."

Burn nurses were a special breed. At Saint Barnabas, they were an eclectic bunch of men and women. They were fifty-five acutely different personalities with one thing in common: the burn unit was in their blood. They were closer to one another than any other group of nurses in the hospital, and because of the impossible stress of their jobs, they were a little bit wilder than any other group as well.

With all the time they spent together in the unit, they knew everything about one another. They knew about Kathy Hetcko's new boyfriend and they knew that Sharon Iossa ate a bowl of mashed potatoes for lunch every day. They gossiped about one another, and they bickered sometimes. They laughed at one another's raunchy jokes and cried on one another's shoulders. One night, on a whim, a group of them finished a tough shift and jumped in a car and drove seven hours to Jamestown, New York, the hometown of their idol, Lucille Ball. They took in all the sights when they got there: the Lucille Ball Little Theatre, the Lucille Ball Memorial Park, the Lucille Ball: Not the Girl Next Door display at the Fenton History Center. Before driving the four hundred miles back, they conspired to collect a souvenir to add to the other Lucy memorabilia sprinkled around the burn unit: the street sign from Lucy Way, which ended up hidden in a storage closet.

All of them had an extreme fear of fire: Sue Manzo had her landlord light her gas grill whenever she wanted to barbecue. Kathe Conlon installed smoke detectors in her garage. None of the nurses put cloths on their tables—that way children couldn't pull on them, overturning hot food or lit candles. And children were simply not allowed in the kitchen when something was cooking. For what they witnessed on an average day, they should have been paid a king's ransom. Instead, they earned between $40,000 and $65,000. But no one was in it for the money.

Mansour said the members of his team could have worked anywhere in the hospital. They were the smartest and most dedicated people in their professions. Like him, they had chosen burns, and most chose to stay. Mansour was part of the reason. It wasn't just that he treated his staff as equals; Hani actually thought of them as equals. There were three things nurses wanted from their job: good pay, flexible hours, and the respect of the doctors they worked with. Most struggled to get the first two; the third was a gift. Rarely did a cardiologist commiserate about a treatment plan with a nurse, or spend time in the nurses' lunchroom, telling jokes or trading diet tips, the way Mansour did.

Within Saint Barnabas, there was a mystery about the burn nurses. They tended to stick together, and they rarely ventured very far from the unit. The average critically ill patient in an intensive care unit received fourteen hours of bedside care per day. Critical burn patients required a nurse at the bedside for twenty-one out of every twenty-four hours. The job was as physically demanding as it was emotionally trying. Not everyone fit in. "You don't get here if you're not good," said Manzo, an eight-year veteran of the burn unit. "If you don't pull your weight, we'll weed you out because you don't belong here." "If you can't become part of the team, you don't last," Kathe Conlon added. In the course of a day, burn nurses could deal with child abuse, elder abuse, or a whole family wiped out by fire. They saw babies scorched into near skeletons and young mothers who were burned beyond recognition trying to save their children. "There are times when this place is so very, very awful, you never want to come back," Manzo confessed. And yet they did.

One morning, as nurses were preparing Alvaro for the tank room, a call came into the unit that a child, burned on more than half his body, was being brought up from the emergency room. Burned children were the worst punishment. Most of the staff had families. For many of them, this case would hit too close to home.

Eight-year-old Jabrill Walker was wheeled into the tank room at 8:15 A.M. Mansour and a team of eight nurses and technicians were waiting. The boy had been playing with matches in his bedroom before school, and his shirt caught fire. Like most freshly burned patients, he was awake and alert, and very frightened. Mansour could see that his burns were grave. "They are almost identical to the Llanos boy's," he concluded, assessing the child's injury. Like Alvaro, little Jabrill would require an escharotomy—cuts down his arms and across his chest to keep the swelling from cutting off his circulation. Manzo was named the charge nurse for the case. She was the single mother of a nine-year-old boy, Anthony, and she talked about him all the time. When she looked down at Jabrill, her hands shook and her face flushed. She saw her own boy's face on the child's burned body.

Jabrill would have to be washed so the doctors could better assess his burns. Manzo pushed Jabrill under the water jets as the others prepared to begin his tanking. "I'm going to tell my mommy what you're doing to me," the child cried. Manzo blinked back tears. "Okay, Jabrill, honey," she said, trying to keep her composure. "We're going to give you a bath now. A big bubble bath." As the hoses dropped from the ceiling, Manzo, her face glistening with perspiration, turned to one of her colleagues. "You coming with that morphine?" she snapped. Then, turning back to the boy, she broke into her son's favorite bathtub song.

Oh, Alice, where are you going?
Upstairs to take a bath.
Alice, with legs like toothpicks,
And a neck like a giraffe.

As the nurses scrubbed, the little boy wailed. Manzo continued to sing.

Alice got in the bathtub.
Alice pulled out the plug.

Jabrill was screaming.

Oh, my gracious! Oh, my soul!
There goes Alice down the hole.
Alice, where are you going?
Blub! Blub! Blub!

With the tanking finally over, Manzo stood in the unit kitchenette, holding a cold soda to her forehead. "I'm on my last thread," she said. Then she broke down in tears.

Most nurses took pride in being stoic. Not in the burn unit. There, no one was afraid to show emotion, and when they did, the others always rallied to support them. Jabrill's case was hardly unusual. In the burn unit, there were hundreds of war stories: the badly burned little girl they nursed back to health, only to read in the newspaper a year later that she had been beaten to death by her parents; the two-year-old boy whose mother had held his face to a steaming radiator; the businesswoman who spent three months recovering from severe burns, then died two years later in a house fire. Burn nurses were asked all the time, "How can you do it? Why do you do it?" The truth was that most of them wouldn't have been happy anywhere else. "The bottom line is, this is where a lot of us belong," Manzo said. In an era when nursing had become more about handing out pills and hooking up IVs, Mansour's nurses clung to the ideal of making a difference. They did the dirty work, and people considered them heroic. They were not unlike soldiers who volunteered for combat: driven by the need to feel worthy and to be a part of something.

So they stayed for one another. They stayed because for every tragedy, there was a success story. They stayed because no one else would.

Chapter 12

Please take me to see my roommate."

Shawn had been awake for a week, and the morphine haze was finally clearing out of his head. He had been plotting to see Alvaro all day. Now it was late at night and his mother had finally gone home. Every time he had asked her about Alvaro, she had said he was fine, okay, getting better every day. The lights in the burn unit were dim, and the respiratory therapist was listening to his breathing. "My roommate is Alvaro Llanos," Shawn said, persisting. "Can you take me to see him?"

The therapist hesitated. He realized that Shawn wasn't about to give up without getting an answer.

"You don't need to worry about him now," the therapist said. "You need to concentrate on yourself."

Shawn had been taken off the critical list that day. His life was out of danger, but he still had a long recovery ahead of him. He promised himself that as soon as he could walk, he would find Al.

The nurses had met few patients as determined as Shawn. Mansour had planned to wean him off the respirator on his third day awake, but Shawn yanked out his breathing tube before Mansour had the chance. On his second day, his feeding tube had been removed and he had asked his girlfriend, Tiha Holmes, for grilled cheese sandwiches. So much of a burn patient's success depended on his psychological makeup. Shawn was smart and he was stubborn— traits that were certain to test the staff but also hasten his own recovery. His face was scarred from second-degree burns, and both of his hands were covered with skin grafts, so he would need extensive physical therapy, but with luck, he would go home in three months, Mansour told Shawn's mother.

Shawn had other ideas. "Give me two weeks and a couple of days, and I'll be out of here," he promised Andy Horvath. "I always set ambitious goals for myself and I usually meet them."

"Why doesn't that surprise me?" Horvath asked rhetorically, and they both laughed.

Shawn took his first steps two days after his late-night request to see Alvaro. A nurse propped him up, keeping her hand under his arm, and led him around his room. He took eight steps, rested a minute, and then took another three. He was shaky and weak and it took all of his concentration to put one foot in front of the other. The next day he felt a little better, but he was discouraged by his overall lack of strength. The day after that, he managed to take fifteen steps on his own, using sheer will. "That's it," the nurse said, clapping her hands. "You're getting better every day."

Shawn hadn't mentioned it, but he was motivated by a single goal: to see his roommate. He also hadn't told anyone that he couldn't sleep at night, wondering why everyone was so vague when he asked about Al. He had started to remember the morning of the fire and how, in his panic, he had turned right out of their third-floor dorm room, toward the elevator he always took downstairs. There was a stairway to the left of their room. He hadn't even thought about it as he fled for his life, and Alvaro had followed him. Had they turned left, they might have escaped the fire unharmed. How would he forgive himself if Alvaro was badly hurt? What if he had died and no one was telling him?

One month after the fire, a nurse asked Shawn if he would like to try to walk to the tank room for his daily treatment. It would be a big step in his recovery, she said. The tank room was twenty-five feet away. *This is my chance,* Shawn said to himself. *My chance to try to see Al.*

With the nurse next to him, Shawn took ten steps to the door of his room, then ten steps down the hallway of the burn ICU. He wasn't sure if he could make it any farther. Those twenty steps had taken him several minutes. His legs were giving out and he was breathing hard. Shawn remembered hearing someone say that Alvaro was three doors down from his room, and he had put that information away for when he needed it. Now he needed to keep moving. He had to keep going. He counted each door he passed. The steps between the rooms seemed like miles.

Finally he reached the third door. Room 4. Shawn turned and glanced through the glass wall. The nurse immediately guided him away. Shawn said nothing, but he had seen what he had wanted to see. He was sorry he had. The patient in the bed was wrapped head-to-toe in gauze and hooked up to a maze of tubes and machines. Shawn recognized the steady whir of the respirator. Then he saw a collage of photographs on the wall. Photographs of Alvaro. Now he knew why everyone had been so evasive: Al was in bad shape.

I should have turned left, Shawn said to himself as the nurse steered him into the tank room. *What was I thinking? Why didn't I turn left?*

Shawn decided he would tell no one what he had seen, not Tiha, not even his mother. He would tell no one of the terrible remorse he felt. But every time he got the chance to pass room 4, he would take it so that he could check in on his friend.

Chapter 13

The day arrived faster than everyone had anticipated—everyone, that is, except Shawn. Christine had always told her son that he could do whatever he wanted to do, be whatever he wanted to be. When Shawn was thirteen, he decided that the street life, and selling drugs and stealing cars and all of the other things that went with it, was a dead end. At the risk of being ridiculed, he walked away from the boys in the neighborhood who had tried so hard to recruit him to their lifestyle, and he never looked back. Having realized that his mother was right, that he could be somebody, and that college was the way to get what he wanted, Shawn hit the books and kept hitting them until his name was on University High's honor roll.

As tenacious as he was proud, Shawn wasn't about to go back on his promise to himself that he would be out of the burn unit in weeks, not the months the doctors had predicted. On a Monday afternoon, days before the staff had thought he would be ready, he left intensive care for step-down. His mother arrived early to escort him on the short walk between the two units. It was a watershed moment, the few steps representing so much in terms of how far Shawn had come on his journey back from the fire. Dressed in a blue hospital gown and slipper socks, with a nurse carrying the oxygen tank that was fitted to a mask over his mouth, Shawn walked the corridor as if in a victory march. Mansour had told Christine that once Shawn awoke from his coma, he would probably progress fairly quickly to step-down. That's when the hard work of recuperation would begin. But no one had expected him to move *this* fast.

"So soon?" Sue Manzo asked as Shawn passed the nurses' station on his way to his new room.

"I told you," Shawn said, grinning.

"Yes, you did," Manzo said.

But Shawn had still not told anyone—not even his mother, and he told his mother everything—that he had seen Alvaro. He had stopped asking about his roommate after he had glimpsed him that first time. He knew no one would tell him the truth. Sure, they were trying to protect him, but they should have known he would find out. Shawn couldn't get Alvaro off his mind, and he couldn't forgive himself for turning the wrong way out of their dorm room, either. He would keep that to himself, too, until he could tell Alvaro that he was sorry, sorry that he had let him down. But every time he passed room 4 and peeked in, nothing seemed to have changed. Alvaro lay there, tubes snaking between bags of fluids and blinking machines and his mummified body, a nurse or doctor always at his side.

Now, walking past room 4, Shawn glanced sideways, looking at the bed where his friend lay motionless, still unconscious. This was Shawn's last chance to look in on his friend; the ICU was behind closed doors, and once he walked through them to the step-down side, he would have no official reason to return except to see Al. After today, he would only be able to wonder about Alvaro—wonder about how he was doing—and Shawn knew he would be wondering about him all day long, from the moment he first woke up in the morning until sleep finally overtook him at night.

"C'mon, Son," Christine said, pulling on Shawn's arm. "This is so exciting, Shawn. We're going to step-down. Before you know it, you'll be home."

"Yeah," Shawn said, trying to sound happy.

The nurses applauded as mother and son passed.

Shawn whimpered like a baby on the morning he was rolled into the OR for surgery on his hands. Pins had to be put in his fingers to immobilize his damaged joints. Otherwise he would lose his fingers. The procedure was relatively easy and would require only local anesthesia, Mansour said. "Aren't you going to knock me out?" Shawn asked, incredulous. "That's not how it's normally done," Mansour answered. "I'm not doing it unless you knock me out," Shawn insisted. Hani relented.

The surgery went as planned, and Shawn was back in his room in two hours. When he woke up from the anesthesia, his mother and Tiha were waiting with pizza. But the next day, Shawn's mood was dark and raw. He complained about his bandaged hands. Eating was awkward, he said. He was having trouble picking up the telephone. His mood wasn't helped by his lack of sleep at night. "What's the trouble?" the nurses asked. It depended on the day, sometimes the hour.

"My forehead stings."

"My fingers ache."

"The skin grafts on my hands are ugly. My mother always said the first thing a woman notices about a man is his hands. Where does that leave me?"

The doctors had said there was no reason Shawn would not, at some point, be able to lead a fairly normal life. His only real physical challenge was getting back the use of his hands, and that would take commitment by him to the painful daily therapy sessions. The therapy, which required the stretching of his taut new skin, would help keep Shawn's hands from constricting and shriveling up. He knew that. But the pain of bending and straightening his fingers was excruciating, and Shawn was finding there were limits to his tolerance and his perseverance. For the first time in his life, he felt powerless. There was nothing he could do to change what had happened. Nothing he could do to erase the scars. No matter how hard he might try or how much he wanted to make something right, his hands would always remind him that there were some things he couldn't control. They would never look better. And he couldn't return to the dorm room and turn left instead of right.

"I need to go to the bathroom," he said one day as the physical therapist pulled and pushed on his bandaged fingers. "I need you to open the door for me."

"No," the therapist said. "You have to at least try to turn the knob yourself."

"Mom?" Shawn asked, looking at Christine, who was seated in a chair near his bed.

"No," the therapist said, looking from Christine to Shawn. "You try, Shawn. You're not doing as much as you should be. You need to start trying harder. You need to start doing things for yourself. If you don't start exercising your hands more, they'll tighten up and you'll lose the use of them. I thought you were a tough guy. Everyone said you were the star patient in ICU. What happened?"

Shawn glared at the therapist.

"Ever have anyone kick you?" Shawn asked through clenched teeth. "Because I'm about to kick you right out of this room."

Christine gasped. This was not the Shawn she knew.

"Shawn!" she snapped. "I've never known you to speak to someone like that. I've never known you to be violent."

"I've never hurt like this before," Shawn responded.

Mansour heard about the incident. He had watched with great hope and admiration as Shawn struggled back to life in the ICU. He had even told his wife, "This boy has the mettle to come all the way back." But now Hani was becoming impatient.

"He is sitting in there like a little king," Mansour griped at a weekly meeting of the burn team. "Everyone is doing everything for him. That's not helping. There's always someone feeding him. Reading to him. I don't know what happened to him. When he was in intensive care, he did everything we asked and more, and he was always so calm and polite. Now he's getting better and he's being impossible."

For her part, Christine was worried about Shawn's state of mind. He had never seemed so angry, so belligerent. Shawn usually handled everything by forgiving and carrying on. But now her easygoing son was a stranger. The more he healed, the more miserable he seemed to become.

In the past, Christine had always known how to make her son feel better. And as recently as a couple of weeks ago, he'd been cheered by the scores of greeting cards he'd received. Schoolchildren from all over the state were sending notes to the Seton Hall students burned in the fire. Christine picked a card from the pile.

"Listen to this one, Shawn," she said, chuckling. The message was written in crayon. "Dear friend," it read. "My name is Evan. I am a Michigan fan. I suppose you like Seton Hall. If you need a good laugh, I strongly suggest the movie *Dumb and Dumber.* Now that is a great movie."

Normally, Shawn would have giggled along with her, but he was stone-faced.

"Humph," he said, turning his attention to the TV.

"Do you want to tell me what's going on?" Christine asked, rubbing her son's head. "Shawn? . . . Shawn?"

Tears rolled down Shawn's cheeks. He wiped them away with his bandaged hand, but they continued to fall, drenching his face and his sheets.

"I guess I'm just getting tired of all this," he said finally.

"But Shawn, you're getting better. You're doing so well. You're alive. We have so much to be thankful for."

"I'm not sleeping, Mom," Shawn said, trying to choke back sobs. "I can't sleep."

"Why, Shawn? What is it? Are you afraid?"

"Mom, I saw Alvaro. I saw him a long time ago. No one would tell me anything about him, so I looked in his room. And I kept looking in after that. I know. I know how sick he is. That's why I don't sleep. I can't sleep because I think he's going to die. And I blame myself. What happened to Al is my fault because I turned the wrong way out of our room."

Shawn's secret was out.

It was a normal Friday night at the Hall. Hundreds of students crowded into the college bar, just down the street from the Seton Hall campus, mingling and drinking three-dollar beers.

Jennifer Lopez's "Waiting for Tonight" was blaring when cops burst through the front door at 1:23 A.M. and swarmed the bar.

"Nobody leaves until we see some ID," one officer shouted. The crowd went quiet.

It had been weeks since the fire, and investigators were frustrated. They were focusing on a small group of students, but no one was talking. The longer the investigation dragged on, the harder it would be to crack the case. Frucci didn't sleep most nights, wondering what to do next. He tossed and turned in his bed, trying to think of ways to move the investigation forward. With the case hopelessly stalled, investigators had finally decided to resort to an old trick, hoping the guise of a raid on underage drinking would shake loose a fresh lead.

One of their chief suspects was Sean Ryan, the kid who had admitted to tearing down the banner, then rushed out of police headquarters, never to return. He had since gotten an attorney and had nothing more to say to investigators. But he had told four different stories to fraternity brothers about where he was when the fire started.

The forensic part of the probe had given up little, except that the fire had started on a couch and had quickly engulfed the entire lounge. It had told investigators that the fire was most likely set, but nothing about who started it. Arson is the hardest crime to prove. According to the International Association of Arson Investigators, arrests are made in only 16 percent of arson cases, and less than 2 percent end in a conviction. Frucci and his team needed people to help them bring this case to justice. But the students who knew things—including Ryan's fraternity brothers—had clammed up after those first interviews. Some had hired lawyers. Others hid behind protective parents when investigators called on them for follow-up interviews. Everyone, it seemed, had circled the wagons.

"We have nothing to move ahead on and won't unless something gives," one law enforcement source told the *Newark Star-Ledger* newspaper.

Frucci and the other investigators had come to see the case in terms of good versus evil, because what kind of kids hid the truth about a crime in which fellow students had died? What kind of people could ruin so many lives, yet continue to live their own as if nothing had happened? Investigators hoped the raid might push something—or someone—into the light.

The Hall was a popular hangout for the Pikes, Ryan's fraternity. The officers had brought with them a dozen grand jury subpoenas naming students who they believed knew more than they were saying.

They corralled a group of students in a back room, many of them Ryan's fraternity brothers, slapped subpoenas in their hands, and walked out.

At least now prosecutors could bring the reluctant students before a grand jury, where they would be asked questions without their parents or their lawyers present—*if* the prosecutor's office could ever make a case strong enough to convene a grand jury.

Chapter 14

Almost two months earlier than the doctors had predicted, Shawn was ready to go home. The snow from the week before had melted and the February day was spring-like, sunny and fifty degrees, as Shawn prepared to leave. The doctors and nurses in the unit were excited. Going home meant a job well done. It was what they looked forward to with every patient. Shawn would have to return to the hospital for therapy every day, but he had progressed to the point where around-the-clock care was no longer necessary. Hani had decided that family support was what Shawn needed most now. The staff had produced a medical miracle; the rest of Shawn's physical and mental recovery would depend on him.

All of the cards Shawn had received, most of them from strangers, had been taken down from the walls and packed up with the rest of his belongings by Christine the night before. His room in step-down, which had been crammed with stuffed animals and flowers and other gifts from well-wishers, was now empty except for his packed bags. Waiting for his parents to come, Shawn sat on his bed, staring at the bare wall, and got lost in his thoughts. He had been in the hospital for a long time and he had made some lifelong friends there. The people in the burn unit had saved his life. As much as he wanted to leave the hospital and go home, some of the staff had come to feel like family and he was sad to leave them.

"We're right here, and you can come back to see us anytime," Chris Ruhren, the director of the burn nurses, told Shawn when she came to say good-bye. Shawn knew that many patients returned to the burn unit, and many kept coming back even years after their treatment had ended; he had met a few of them while he was there. But he wasn't so sure he wanted to be one of them. As much as he had become attached to people on the staff, he wanted to be able to put the fire behind him someday. He knew that would take time—at least until after Alvaro was out of the woods—but he didn't want to live his life as "one of the victims of the Seton Hall fire."

Christine arrived with Kenny on the second floor with a camera and directed everyone to pose for pictures. Shawn and the nurses, hugging. Shawn and Dr. Mansour, grinning from ear to ear. "We're going to put together a whole album," Christine said.

"You've done very well," Mansour said, hugging Shawn.

"I'm sorry I was so difficult sometimes," Shawn said. "I'm grateful for everything you did for me. Thank you."

"Save a copy of that picture for me," Mansour said. "I'm going to put it on my desk."

"You have a great son," nurse Eileen Gehringer told Christine, and the women hugged.

"We love you all," Christine said.

Gehringer handed Shawn his discharge order: Percocet for pain. Benadryl for itch. Xanax for anxiety. Eye salve. Sleeping pills. "And every day downstairs for therapy," she said. "That's the most important thing."

"I know. I know," Shawn said.

"Are you ready to go, Shawn?" Christine asked.

"Let's go, son," Kenny said.

But Shawn hesitated. "There's something I have to do first," he said.

Christine and Kenny followed as Shawn led the way. He walked slowly out of step-down and down the hall toward the double doors leading to the burn ICU. Christine wasn't surprised. The double doors swung open and Shawn made his way across the unit toward room 4, Alvaro's room.

At that moment, Alvaro was being rolled out of his room on a gurney to be taken for his daily tanking. Shawn stopped when he saw his roommate. He braced himself against the wall as the gurney approached, feeling as if the floor were moving beneath him. He looked down at Alvaro, lying there motionless, and the room seemed to swirl around him. Alvaro looked no different, no better, than he had on Shawn's last day in the ICU, the last time Shawn had been able to peek into his room.

Shawn blinked and took a big gulp of air to regain his equilibrium. All these weeks later, and Alvaro was still unconscious. Blood and brownish fluids oozed through his gauze body armor.

It was just as Shawn had feared. Day after day in step-down he had fantasized about Alvaro bursting into his room, smiling his big, white smile, saying, *Look, Shawn, I'm getting better! I'm really getting better. Let's see who makes it to the finish line first.* But dreams were dreams, and Alvaro wasn't improving at all. *Will he ever get better?* Shawn wondered. "Al," he said, reaching for his roommate, then quickly retreating as the gurney carrying the sickest patient in the burn unit pushed past.

Christine and Kenny enveloped Shawn and started to lead him away, but Shawn pulled back.

"No," he said, standing his ground. "No. I need to see him before I leave."

Shawn took a seat in the nurses' break room, across from the tank room, so he could see when Alvaro was wheeled back out. His parents sat with him. No one spoke. Thirty minutes passed. Christine and Kenny made small talk. *What a perfect day outside. Did you happen to see in the paper that . . . ?* Shawn said nothing. Another thirty minutes went by. Finally the doors to the tank room swung outward and the rolling gurney carrying Alvaro emerged. His gauze was white again, but it wouldn't be long before the blood seeped through. The exhausted nurses pushed on. Shawn waited as they counted to three and then lifted Alvaro's limp body from the gurney onto his bed in room 4. Alvaro had been big to begin with, but he looked like a giant lying there.

With Alvaro settled in, Shawn pulled on a yellow smock, rubber gloves, a head cap, and a face mask from the cart outside the room. The protective gear was required to help shield Alvaro from outside germs and deadly infections. The nurses exchanged furtive glances as Shawn approached. How would he handle this? Could he handle it? Christine watched through the glass as Shawn walked into the room and stood over his comatose roommate. She couldn't help feeling pride. Her son was a good boy. A caring boy. She really believed he would trade places with Alvaro if he could. She was thankful that he couldn't.

Shawn studied Alvaro's face. All he could see were his mouth and his eyes, and his eyes were closed.

"He can hear you if you talk to him," a nurse said.

The lonely drone of the respirator filled the room. Shawn couldn't speak. Instead, he bowed his head and began to pray silently. *Please, God, let Alvaro live. Let me help him get through this. Give my friend the same chance you gave me.* Then, in utter grief, Shawn broke down. His shoulders heaved and his sobs were deep and mournful. He tore off his gown and ran from the room, into his mother's open arms. How could he leave Alvaro? How could he abandon him this way? He needed to tell him, *Al, you're going to pull through this. It will take a little longer, but you will pull through. I'm not really leaving you. I promise you I'll be here to see you through this, no matter how long it takes.* But Alvaro couldn't hear him; Shawn was sure of it. He wondered if he would ever get the chance to tell Al that he cared about him more than he had ever cared about almost anyone except his own family.

"Let's go home now, baby boy," Christine said, pulling a tissue from her purse and leading her son away.

"Oh, Mom," he cried. "What is going to happen to Al?"

Chapter 15

Shawn had been home from the hospital three days when death began to close in on his college roommate.

Alvaro had been showing slight signs of improvement in recent days. Then, overnight, his temperature shot up to 105. His blood pressure and heart rate were dropping, and his respiratory system was failing. After weeks of hanging to life by a thread, Alvaro was dying.

Mansour suspected a catastrophic infection was building in his lungs. He ordered X-rays. They suggested acute respiratory distress syndrome. If it was going to happen, ARDS usually occurred within the first few weeks of burn treatment. It was an insidious adversary, stiffening the lungs of patients and literally stealing their breath until even a respirator couldn't work hard enough to keep them alive. The low levels of oxygen in their blood often caused massive organ failure. The mortality rate for ARDS was high. A third or more of burn patients died from it, and Alvaro was already so sick . . .

As the news spread, the burn unit turned as gloomy as the raw, rainy late-winter weather. The burn team took it personally when one of their patients took a turn for the worse. Alvaro had fought a valiant fight, and it was a miracle he had lived this long. But even though Alvaro's prognosis was grim, they weren't about to give up on him. "We don't lose eighteen-year-olds here," Susan Manzo vowed as she washed out Alvaro's mouth. "Uh-uh. *Not here.*"

If only that were true.

Even Alvaro's parents realized their son was on the brink of death. "Why is his fever so high?" Daisy had asked when her son's temperature suddenly spiked. "He is getting sicker," a nurse said. "We're not sure why yet." Daisy had screamed with grief until her husband could only shake her to make her stop, and then she had sobbed, "Why? Why is he getting sicker when he is supposed to be getting better?" Daisy's conflicting emotions were tearing her apart. Christine had taken Shawn home and he was walking and even talking about going back to school. Shawn was getting on with his life, and Daisy was glad for that. She really was. But what about Alvaro? "¿Por qué Dios no está tomando cuidado de nuestro hijo?" she cried. *Why isn't God taking care of our son?*

The Llanoses' life had been one long string of ill fortune since two years earlier, when Alvaro senior had awoken one night with a vicious headache and then watched in the bathroom mirror as the left side of his face involuntarily contorted into a grimace. For three months, he fought back from his stroke, and even then he had only partially recovered. His speech was permanently affected and he still walked with the aid of a cane. He had reluctantly given up his factory job at the Marcal Paper Mills in Elmwood Park, where he had worked nights as a foreman on the production line. Daisy quit her day job as a clerk at the Paterson post office, where she sorted mail, to take care of her sick husband. The family had never had a lot of money before that, but with both parents working, they had been able to make ends meet. After the stroke, what had been hard became harder.

Family had always been more important than material possessions to Daisy and Alvaro senior. They drove a beat-up Acura and lived in a low-income section of Paterson, a withering city whose claim to fame was that it had once been home to the American Industrial Revolution. But their apartment was spotless and it was decorated with religious icons in the china closet and framed photographs of Jesus on the walls. Their home was within a few blocks of their large extended family, and family get-togethers were a mainstay of life.

On weekends, dozens of aunts, uncles, and cousins gathered on a tiny patch of asphalt outside the Llanoses' back door for afternoon cookouts or Sunday dinners. While the women prepared feasts of lasagna and barbecued chicken and rice and beans in Daisy's kitchen, the children played dominoes or basketball outside, and the men sat on the back porch drinking Corona and talking about *béisbol* and *fútbol*.

Once in a while, Mr. and Mrs. Llanos had gone to a salsa club in the city and danced the night away. After twenty years of marriage, they still had a sparkle in their eyes when they looked at each other. They were gentle people who took joy in simple things. But after Mr. Llanos's stroke, everything had changed. Life for the family had become a series of doctor's visits and financial worries. Insurance bills piled up. With no steady income, they became dependent on Social Security checks, hardly enough to sustain a family of five. Alvaro took on two part-time jobs—one as a stock boy in a bird store, and another as an orderly in a nursing home—to help out his parents. When he wasn't studying, he was working, doing all he could to ease his parents' burden.

Daisy was a worrier by nature. After her husband's stroke, she rarely slept. Her nerves in tatters, she had fallen into a deep depression that couldn't be shaken even with pills. She wondered what her family had done to anger God. Still, every day, she had picked herself up and walked to Saint Joseph's Roman Catholic Church in Paterson to give thanks for her good fortune: her husband was alive; her daughters, Shirley, then twenty-five, and Shany, sixteen, were healthy; and young Alvaro—well, he was the greatest blessing of all.

There was something special about Alvaro. Everyone who met him felt it. He was disarmingly shy and sweet, the kind of kid who was always sticking up for the underdog, even though he was part of the popular crowd. When other boys picked on the class nerd, Alvaro came to his defense. He never stood in the hallways between classes, cruelly poking fun at the fat girls, the way his friends sometimes did.

Alvaro could have had any girl he wanted at John F. Kennedy High, but he never had a girlfriend before he met Angie at the start of their senior year. *He's almost too good to be true,* Angie thought when she met him. Other girls thought so, too, but their bashful classmate was more interested in baseball than in girls.

Indeed, baseball was Alvaro's passion, and he had shown a real talent for it. He had started out in the peewee league and then moved to the midgets and onto a citywide team. Before the fire, he had intended to try out for the Seton Hall team and dreamed of one day playing for his beloved Mets. Some of his coaches along the way had said he was good enough to realize his dream. But first he had to finish college, his parents had said. Education was more important than sports. Education was everything. Alvaro agreed.

Alvaro was one of nine male cousins who grew up together in Paterson and the first person in his large, extended family to go to college. His cousins, even the older ones, looked up to him, and he took the responsibility of being a role model seriously. Other students skipped classes to go to the beach, but not Alvaro. His studies came before everything except the needs of his parents. Even on weekends, he shut himself in his bedroom, asking his family not to disturb him until his homework was finished. Alvaro was going to make something of himself—he had promised his parents he would. And once he did, he would buy his mother the home she had always dreamed of having.

"How can I blame God for wanting him?" Daisy said when describing her son to one of his nurses. But the thought of losing Alvaro was so traumatic for Daisy that the burn nurses feared she was headed for a nervous breakdown. The longer Alvaro didn't show progress, the more unpredictable she became, sulking one minute, smiling the next. She had become quick to anger, usually about things that didn't matter. Alvaro senior held in all his fears because he wanted to spare his wife any more stress, but he, too, was in turmoil. Sometimes the pain in his head got so bad that he thought he was having another stroke, but he kept even those times to himself. Thinking they were sparing each other, the couple simply avoided speaking to each other about their son. Day after day, they drove to the hospital early in the morning, listening to the radio rather than talking. Then they passed the hours in Alvaro's room, watching sports on TV or reading the Bible.

As the days passed and Alvaro continued to hover between life and death, the two shut out the world, even the warnings from the medical staff about the precariousness of their son's situation. "He's fighting, but he's very sick," the nurses would say, and Daisy and Alvaro senior would stare at them blankly or nod their heads. They asked the same irrelevant questions day after day.

When will Alvaro wake up?

Were his eyes damaged in the fire?

Will he ever be the same? Will he ever look the way he did?

Daisy was a young forty years old, so much so that before Alvaro was burned, people often mistook her for the sister of her eldest daughter, Shirley. But she now seemed to age dramatically with each passing day. Her mouth turned down in a perpetual frown, and deep, dark circles scooped out the soft flesh under her eyes.

When her husband was sick, she had sought the help of a psychologist to cope. Susan Fischer, the burn unit social worker, had tried to counsel Daisy. Nothing had helped this time. If only she could hear Alvaro's voice, she told the nurses, she would feel better. If only she could be assured that he heard her when she spoke to him. *Bebito, I love you. Mommy is here.* If only she could sleep next to him so he wouldn't be afraid. The nurses listened patiently. *There is always someone with Alvaro,* they would say, trying to soothe Daisy's frayed nerves. *Save your strength for when he wakes up. That's when he'll need you.*

But such reassurances only went so far with Daisy. Alvaro was always so proud of himself and the way he looked. He liked to wear shorts and short-sleeved shirts to show off his attractive brown body. *Will he ever look good in his shorts and his short-sleeved shirts again?* she would ask. The nurses would shake their heads and wonder how Daisy could be discussing her son's looks when it was still so uncertain whether he would even survive. But Daisy refused to think about life without Alvaro, or if she did, she was keeping those thoughts buried in a deep and inaccessible place.

There were occasional moments of lucidity. Once, she stood at the pay phone in the hallway outside the burn unit, commiserating with relatives and friends. "No quiero que mi hijo muera," she cried bitterly. *I don't want my son to die.* Alvaro senior always hovered nearby. "Oh, please, God! No!" he pleaded. "Please! I want him to wake up now." But mostly the two parents cultivated a fog of denial and sunk deep into the hole of optimism.

Fischer told a meeting of the burn team that she was worried about the couple. "The family is in hell," Fischer reported to the staff. "This is their golden child and he's not getting better. They are looking for answers to comfort them—answers we can't give them. She's not sleeping at all. He's not sleeping at all. They don't sleep because they are constantly expecting the phone to ring in the middle of the night. Even sleeping medications aren't working. It's just an impossible situation, really."

"I don't know what to tell them anymore," Hani said, but what he was thinking was, *Whatever I tell them, they don't seem to grasp it. I'm not sure if it's a language barrier or denial, but I suspect it's a little of the first and a lot of the second.*

In mid-March, with Alvaro still teetering between life and death, the situation reached the breaking point. Mansour and his colleagues, burn surgeons Sylvia Petrone and Michael Marano, were standing at the nurses' station outside Alvaro's room. The doctors were discussing Alvaro's deteriorating condition and what more they could do to try to reverse it, when the couple approached them and began their daily inquisition. "What is the tear in Alvaro's eyelid?" Daisy asked accusingly. "And what is the small sore on his leg?" Petrone, who tended to be direct, decided it was time to jolt Alvaro's parents into reality. The Llanoses had to be prepared for their son to die.

"Look," Petrone said, clearly agitated, "don't worry about his eye or the thing on his leg. He's very, very sick. He's in critical condition. The other things don't matter right now. At this point we're trying to keep him *alive*. We'll deal with the other things later. Do you understand?"

Daisy collapsed in tears. "Why aren't you making him better?" she cried. "Why aren't you helping him? Why?" As the doctors stood there, with no words left to say, Daisy turned and ran from the burn unit with Alvaro senior close behind her.

Mansour had seen parents break down before. The burn unit was the last place in the world a parent wanted a child to be. But Alvaro needed his family to be strong. Family support often meant the difference between life and death in the burn unit. Mansour knew that Daisy and Alvaro senior would be beyond consoling if they lost their son. Of course they would. But he worried more about whether they could cope if their boy lived. How would they cope with having a burned son?

Turning to look in on his sickest patient, Mansour found himself feeling suddenly miserable. "Poor boy," he said, talking to himself. "He is fighting so hard. He wants so much to live, and his parents are doing everything they can to be supportive. But they are losing their grip."

Chapter 16

The nurses in the burn unit marveled at Alvaro's girlfriend, Angie. They listened when she whispered in his ear: "I'm here, baby. It's Angie. I love you. I miss you. I'll be right here when you wake up." They watched as she closed her eyes, pretending to be someplace else, gently rubbing lotion on his swollen brown feet, the only part of him she could touch. "Where are you today?" the nurses would ask. "We're on a Caribbean island," Angie would say. Or "We're floating on a big white cloud." They read her letters, notes written in a big, curly scrawl and taped to the wall at the foot of Alvaro's bed so that he would see them, Angie explained, if he suddenly woke up and she wasn't there. Sometimes the nurses felt like voyeurs because the letters were so achingly personal, the words of an idealistic young girl desperately in love: "I love you, baby. I love you so much. We will never be apart. Never. God is taking care of you, and I know that when you come out of this, God will give me the strength to take care of you."

Angie was petite and pretty, with wavy auburn hair and mahogany eyes. The nurses often told her, "Angie, you're more devoted than most of the husbands and wives of our patients." Privately, they were taking bets about how long she would last. The nurses had seen families break down from the strain of dealing with burns and the time it took for patients to recover. They had seen wives leave husbands because they couldn't deal with disfigurement, and husbands walk out on wives rather than stick out the long and difficult process of burn recovery.

The first signs of strain began to surface when Alvaro had been in a coma for nearly two months. Angie came to visit on a Sunday afternoon, after missing a day, which everyone, especially Daisy, had noticed because Angie never missed a day. Her eyes were red and puffy from crying, and her hair hung limply over her shoulders. She usually wore her hair pulled up in a spirited ponytail. She seemed agitated and distracted, not the happy girl who was always trying to cheer up everyone else.

Daisy greeted Angie with a hug, the way she always did. Angie sat next to Alvaro's bed and stared at his face. *Why doesn't he do something, anything, to let me know he's here?* she wondered. *Why can't he give a sign that he hears me?* As always, Alvaro just lay there, dead to the world, his only movement the rise and fall of his chest as the respirator pushed air into and out of his lungs.

Angie paced around the room for a while, reading and rereading the same cards and letters that people had sent

Alvaro, and then left earlier than usual, though not before Daisy asked her what the rush was. Making some excuse about a cousin's birthday that she couldn't miss or her father would be angry, Angie fled out the door. One of the nurses caught up with her in the hallway.

"Are you okay?" the nurse asked, patting Angie's back.

"I hate coming here," Angie said through gritted teeth. "When you come here every day and you don't see any change, it's discouraging. It all seems so hopeless. I know he's not going to wake up for at least another month, and my body is exhausted."

"Go home and get some rest," the nurse said. "It's okay to take care of yourself, Angie."

"But his parents will be mad at me," Angie said.

"His parents will have to understand," the nurse said.

A few days later, Angie arrived at the hospital, more agitated than before. She had skipped two visits that week. She would not be coming quite as much now, she explained, almost apologetically, to the nurse in the room. Getting a ride to the hospital from Seton Hall wasn't easy, Angie said. Besides that, she had schoolwork to do, which took up most of her time. And she hadn't been to the gym in weeks. She was just so tired. Of course, the nurse said, looking at Angie knowingly.

Angie said she loved Alvaro, but she was starting to despise the hospital. The putrid smells. The hiss of the respirator. She didn't want to start hating Alvaro, too. If only he would talk to her, comfort her. He had always been able to make her feel better, to calm her when she was afraid.

"Take a deep breath," the nurse said.

The day had begun badly for her, Angie explained, and she started to cry. All of her friends were out doing things—fun things—and she was in her room, listening to music and thinking about everything that had happened. It was as if she had to live two different lives now. In school she talked and laughed with her friends. But then she felt ashamed for having fun when Alvaro was fighting for his life, so she would transform herself into the dutiful girlfriend, spending hours at the side of her comatose boyfriend, hating every minute of it. Angie wanted to live her life, not be trapped in a burn unit. "What's so wrong about that?" she asked defensively. "I'm a young girl, and young girls are supposed to have fun, right? Right?"

"Right," the nurse said, nodding sympathetically.

As if the day wasn't dark enough, Angie saw some of Alvaro's wounds for the first time. The doctors had removed the bandages from his legs that morning so that his donor sites—places where patches of healthy skin had been shaved off his thighs and calves for grafting onto his chest and back—could heal better. Alvaro's legs looked like a checkerboard of red, raw flesh. Angie had been stunned by the sight. "Will it get better than this?" she asked with fear in her voice. "It will get better," the nurse said. "But the scars will never disappear." *What's going to happen when she sees his burns?* the nurse wondered. The injuries to Alvaro's back and chest had been catastrophic. His torso didn't even look human.

Angie felt as if her head would explode. She hadn't wanted to admit it, even to herself, but she had been worrying lately about the way Alvaro would look. In high school he had been nominated one of the best-looking boys in their senior class, and he was also voted best dressed. He had always taken pride in his appearance. He wore only brand names. And as shy as he was, he loved to make an entrance. "Baby, do you think I'm cute?" he would sometimes ask Angie before they walked into a club or a party. "Baby, you're gorgeous," she would tell him. Angie loved being seen with Alvaro. He was a real catch. In high school, all the girls were jealous when he chose her as his girl. How would it be now? Angie wondered.

"It scares me a little—what he's going to look like," Angie told a friend one day. "He was always so self-conscious. I know how he is. He won't be the same person."

People were asking too much of her, Angie went on. Especially Alvaro's parents. "They expect me to be here all the time like they are," she said. "They expect me to be the perfect girlfriend. They expect me to be a wife, but we're not even married."

Then Angie revealed a story from her past. In 1995, she said, when she was twelve years old, her father was trapped in a burning car. His face and hands were horribly burned. For a year after he left the hospital, he hid at home rather than face the stares of strangers. He couldn't even look at himself, so he took down all the mirrors in the house. When he finally did go out, people stared, just as he had feared,

Angie said. She wanted to shout at them, *Stop looking! What is the matter with you?* But she quietly endured her father's discomfort. It was her discomfort, too, Angie admitted. "Little kids would point. I saw it."

"I think people think I can handle this with Alvaro better because I've been through it," Angie said. "But I think it makes it harder, knowing what I know."

She worried that she might not be able to stick it out with Alvaro. "I'm not proud of that, so I try not to think about it, but say he has a big operation and he wants me there for him and I have a big calculus test the next day. I'm eighteen," said Angie, whose tears turned to sobs. "I'm supposed to be with my friends, chilling and going shopping, and I'm going to be here in the hospital with my sick boyfriend? My life hasn't been easy. But when I got to college, I was so happy. Everything was perfect. Then this happened and it all just fell apart. Am I going to be able to help him through this? I just don't know."

On the third day of spring, Alvaro's fever broke.

"This is the turning point we have been waiting for," Mansour told Daisy and Alvaro senior. After three weeks of trying to keep Alvaro alive, the doctors had finally gotten the edge in the battle against the infection that was killing him. If his temperature remained normal for the next couple of days, they would be back in the business of healing him.

Daisy smiled for the first time in weeks. "¡Gracias a Dios!" she cried, burying her head in her husband's shoulder. *Thanks be to God.*

"God is helping the doctors to save our son," Alvaro senior added.

Alvaro's fever stayed away the next day, and the day after that, so Mansour ordered his medications to be cut back. The heavy doses of morphine he had been given since the fire had kept Alvaro comatose, and another drug, Norcuron, had kept him paralyzed. By backing off the medication, Alvaro should soon begin showing signs of life, Mansour said.

For days afterward, Daisy sat by her son's side, looking for something, anything, to indicate he was waking up. *"Bebito,"* she whispered, "I know you can hear me. If you can, give me a sign." But nothing changed. Alvaro lay there, flat on his back, his eyes sewn partially shut, white gauze wrapping all but his feet and a patch of his face. She began to lose hope again.

Still, she returned. One Tuesday afternoon, seventy-five days after the fire, she squeezed Alvaro's hand and purred with her usual reassurances. "Alvaro, Mommy is here. If you can hear me, give me a sign, my darling."

Her son blinked.

"Blink again," Daisy cried. "Alvaro, honey, please blink again for Mommy!" She was terrified that her eyes had merely played a cruel trick.

A few seconds passed.

Alvaro's sutured eyelids flickered again.

Daisy ran to the nurses' station. "My son—," she cried, "he is waking up! I saw him blink."

Two of the nurses returned with Daisy to Alvaro's room. This time, when Daisy asked him to respond, nothing happened. She asked again. Nothing. He probably went back to sleep, the nurses said. Privately, though, the staff chalked it up to a mother's desperation. The nurses hadn't seen any signs from Alvaro, and even if he was coming out of his coma, it was unlikely he could comprehend orders. It would take weeks before he was clearheaded enough to understand commands.

But not every nurse was so quick to discount Daisy's testimony. Ann Marie Majestic, who had been with Alvaro from the beginning, started to talk to her patient on the off chance that he really had responded to his mother. Majestic was fiercely protective and possessive of Alvaro. Once, she yanked the curtain closed around his bed when a man who was visiting another patient stopped to stare. "This isn't a circus act," she had snapped. The man had slinked away.

Majestic had been burned as a child when a boiler exploded and scalded her right leg. She still had the scars to show for it. That experience was the main reason she chose burns as a specialty, and she had firsthand experience of what her patients were going through.

Two days after Daisy claimed she'd seen Alvaro blink, Majestic thought she saw something, too. She was talking to Alvaro as she washed his burns in the tank room. "You're in the hospital because there was a fire on campus. We're taking care of you. It's all right, honey. You're on a machine that is helping you to breathe, and your eyes are stitched to protect them." Alvaro's breathing suddenly quickened, so Majestic chattered on. "Angie got out of the dorm without injury.

Shawn's okay. And you're doing better. Do you understand what I'm saying, honey?"

Ever so slightly, Alvaro nodded.

"You hear me, honey?"

He nodded again.

Majestic had watched Alvaro struggle to live for weeks. When she went home each day, she wondered whether he would be there when she came back. About the only thing he had going for him was his age. His lungs were damaged, and a host of potentially menacing infections festered in his system. His burns still bled so badly that he needed regular blood transfusions, sometimes two a day. A thirty-year-old with the same injuries wouldn't have had a chance. Majestic admired Alvaro's grit. His family had told her how shy he was, how humble, but no one had to tell her about his spirit. Alvaro still faced daunting odds, but his will to live was powerful.

"You're getting better, honey," Majestic said, and the other nurses and technicians in the room quietly wiped away their tears.

Two flights down, Shawn was about to reach another milestone in his recovery. He was finishing up his last session with Roy Bond, his physical therapist. Bond was a bear of a man with a barrel chest and hands the size of dinner plates. He had started his career at Saint Barnabas twenty-seven years earlier, in the hospital's linen department, then studied at night to get his degree in physical therapy. Bond was as warm as he was large, and he was genuinely attached to his patients—and they to him. He could get patients to do anything with his smooth, persuasive voice. Shawn was no exception.

It was partly because of Bond that Shawn had kept his promise to return to the hospital every day for physical therapy. When he had started, weeks earlier, he hadn't been able to take ten steps on level ground without getting so winded he needed to rest. Now he could climb four flights of stairs and pedal a stationary exercise bicycle for twenty minutes straight without becoming exhausted. Shawn still tired more easily than normal, but it would be up to him to regain the rest of his strength.

"Turn out the lights! The party's over," Bond said. "What's that song they used to sing? 'It's so hard to say goodbye'?"

Bond tried not to seem sad, but in a way, he was. Shawn had come a long way in a few weeks. They had worked hard together. They had laughed and cried together. Now Shawn was on his way to the next phase of his recovery, a phase that would decide his future. He had passed boot camp, and now the real test began—the test that would determine whether he would live his life as a burn victim or as a man.

The two hugged before Shawn turned to leave the physical therapy room after his final session.

"Love you, Roy," Shawn said.

"Love you, too, kid," Bond said, pushing Shawn toward the door—pushing him so that Shawn wouldn't see that he was crying.

Shawn was melancholy as he left Bond behind and headed upstairs to the burn unit to look in on Alvaro. Here he was, celebrating another milestone in his recovery. He should be happy. But how could he be happy when Alvaro wasn't getting better?

Shawn steeled himself as he walked toward Alvaro's room. Nearly three months had passed since that frigid Wednesday in January, when he and Alvaro were awakened in the middle of the night by the sound of the fire alarm and crawled out of their room into the dark, smoky third-floor hallway in Boland Hall. He missed his roommate. Missed his incessant teasing about the Yankees, and his contagious chuckle. Missed the way he tidied up his room like a girl and always wore a baseball cap.

"Hurry and come inside!" the nurse cried when she saw Shawn coming. "Come in and talk, because he can hear you!"

Shawn could hardly believe it. Goose bumps popped up on his arms, and his whole body tingled with anticipation. He pulled on the gown and gloves and rushed to his friend's bedside. "Al! It's Shawn. What's up?" he said. His hands trembled.

Alvaro blinked slowly, unmistakably.

Shawn's eyes widened. "It's okay," he continued breathlessly. He wasn't sure what to say next. He hadn't been expecting this. Alvaro could hear him. He could even respond. "I'm okay," Shawn said, talking faster than he could think. "I'm going to get Mets tickets so we can see a game . . . Al . . . you're going to be okay . . . you've been through a lot . . . but I'm going to be right here for you. I'm going to be right here."

Alvaro blinked harder. Shawn's eyes filled up.

"He hears me," he said, wiping away the tears with the back of his gloved hand. "That's why he's trying to blink—to let me know he hears me."

Alvaro blinked again.

Chapter 17

Ten days had passed with no sign of Angie. She had told Daisy she was going to Puerto Rico for spring break, which Daisy thought was curious. *What kind of girl leaves for vacation when the boy she loves is fighting for his life in a burn unit?* she thought to herself. *This is not the Angie I know, the girl Alvaro loves.*

Angie had said she needed to get away. She hadn't slept through the night in weeks and her nerves were frayed. What good would she be to anyone if she fell apart? She had promised Daisy she would visit Alvaro the day before she left for her trip, but she hadn't come. Then she called again on the day she got back, never mentioning the fact that she went away without saying good-bye, and said she would be at the hospital in an hour or so. So Daisy waited, watching for the unit's double doors to swing open and her son's diminutive girlfriend to skip through, her ponytail swaying back and forth. She watched the doors for minutes, then hours. No Angie.

The next day, Angie finally showed up. Daisy and Alvaro senior were rubbing lotion on Alvaro's feet when she came in. Angie arrived in Alvaro's room with a copper tan, her thick, auburn hair, sun-bleached with streaks of pale blond, cascading over her shoulders. She still wore Alvaro's crucifix ring on a chain around her neck, along with her own matching crucifix ring on her left hand. Daisy took that as a good sign. The forced smile on Angie's face, however, was not.

"Hola," Angie said, hugging Daisy. Then she greeted Alvaro senior. "¿Cómo estas?" *How are you?*

Hurrying to get through her excuses, Angie apologized for not coming earlier. She hadn't felt well, she said—maybe too much time in the sun, maybe the bumpy airplane flight, maybe a virus or something—and she still had tons of homework to catch up on. Daisy was angry at Angie, especially after her daughters said they suspected that Angie was "checking out" on Alvaro. But maybe her daughters were wrong. Now that she was back, everything would be better. "Entiendo," Daisy said warmly to Angie. *I understand.*

Daisy continued to massage Alvaro's feet, and Angie chattered on, barely taking a breath between words. The weather in Puerto Rico had been warm and sunny. The island was paradise, the ocean turquoise, just as it looked in the travel brochures, and the people were *maravillosa*. She didn't know there could be so many friendly people in one place. She hadn't wanted to come back, not so soon, or—what she didn't say—maybe not ever.

"What's new around here?" Angie asked brightly.

No one told her about Alvaro's waking up. They wanted Angie to be surprised. Alvaro had not stirred the whole time she chattered away. Angie was standing at his side, but her face was turned toward Daisy and Alvaro senior, who were still at his feet. Now, he raised his left arm off the bed, slowly but deliberately. Daisy glanced at her son, then at Angie, who had started to say, "Have you seen Shawn lately?" before stopping midsentence and turning toward Alvaro. A long second passed. Alvaro raised his right arm. Angie's eyes flew wide open. Then he raised both arms, this time higher and more dramatically, a motion that said, *Angie, I'm here. I'm alive. And I hear you.*

The people in the room held their breath, each afraid to exhale for fear the moment would pass too quickly and be gone forever.

Angie broke the stillness.

"Al?" she asked incredulously, breathlessly. "Baby, can you hear me?"

Alvaro moved his fully extended arms, faster this time, up and down, up and down. The heart monitor bleeped from the jump in his heart rate. Angie placed her hand gently on his. She looked down at his bandaged face. His eyes were still partially stitched shut, and she knew he couldn't really see her, not clearly. His mouth was exposed and he was trying to speak, but he couldn't because there was a breathing tube stuck in his throat. He formed words with his lips, but Angie couldn't understand what he was trying to say.

"He's trying to tell me something," Angie cried.

"Talk to him," Daisy said. This was the first time she had seen Alvaro try to speak.

Angie talked about her brother's birthday party. The whole family was there, kids and all, and there were balloons and a big chocolate cake with thick buttercream frosting, "your favorite." She talked about the shameful grade she had gotten on a calculus test, an 84. "I could kill myself for getting that grade," she said. "Can you believe it?" She talked about the computer lab at school. She was spending a lot of time there, the way they had done together, but it wasn't nearly as much fun without him. "I love you," Angie said. "And I miss you."

Alvaro's mouth was forming indecipherable words. One after the other after the other. All silent, none of them comprehensible.

"He's talking. He's talking, but I don't understand," Angie whispered hoarsely. "It's been so long since I've been able to talk to you!" she cried. "And I have so many stories to tell you."

Tears spilled out of Alvaro's eyes, dampening the gauze mask that bandaged the rest of his face.

"Look!" Alvaro senior cried. "He is crying. Don't cry, Pápi, please don't cry."

Daisy was crying, too, crying because she was seeing the first emotion from her son in months. As much as she hated to see her son weep, she loved that he was feeling something, and knowing her son as she did, she knew what it was.

"Let him cry," Daisy said. "His tears are the only way he can tell us what he is feeling, and he is feeling love."

So the boy who had been given a one-in-three chance of living, who had been on the verge of death only weeks before, cried.

Chapter 18

"Hello. Hello. Hello." The words spilled out of Alvaro's mouth like a river released from the ice after a spring thaw. A moment earlier, Michael Marano, a burn surgeon, had removed the breathing tube from Alvaro's trachea, allowing him to speak for the first time since the morning of the fire. It had been ninety days. "Okay, Alvaro, come on now, can you say something to us?" Marano had asked. Eager to test his new freedom, Alvaro didn't hesitate. *Hello. Hello. Hello.*

The first words had been a long time coming. First, Alvaro had to be weaned from the respirator that had kept him alive for the past thirteen weeks. Little by little, the settings had been lowered, decreasing the volume of oxygen the machine pushed into his fragile lungs. Every adjustment forced him to work harder to breathe with the machine. Then he was taken off the respirator completely for short spurts of time, forcing him to do all the work himself, pulling air into his lungs, pushing it out. At first, it was fifteen minutes. Then an hour. Then two hours. The process was exhausting. Sometimes he felt as if he were suffocating as his lungs struggled to do what the machine had done so effortlessly, and no amount of reassurance from the nurses or the respiratory therapists could completely calm him. At times, Alvaro slept the rest of the day after a particularly grueling session off the vent. "You have to work harder," the therapists would tell him. "Once you're off the vent, the healing will go faster. The quicker you'll be able to go home." *Home,* Alvaro would say to himself, then drag in another mouthful of air and blow it out again. Finally, ten days after the tube was removed for the first time, the machine was put away. The sickest patient in the burn unit was ready to breathe on his own.

Alvaro's throat was swollen and raw. His voice was tentative and his speech robotic. But to the doctors, the hellos spilling from the boy's lips were melodious. Those first words, though fleeting, said everything. Alvaro had survived merciless odds, and his eagerness to communicate told them how much he yearned to return to life.

Once Alvaro started speaking that morning, he didn't stop.

"It feels good to talk."

"Please wipe my eyes."

"The TV, please."

"Cream for my lips."

Shawn arrived in Alvaro's room for his regular noon visit after his occupational therapy. No one had told him his friend was talking.

"Al, how you doin'?" he began, as he did every day.

"Chillin'," Alvaro replied, the word spoken softly but deliberately.

Shawn did a double take. "What did you say?"

"Chillin'," Alvaro said again, this time with more force.

Shawn wanted to shout with happiness and relief. He knew how important it was for Alvaro to be able to communicate, how much it meant in terms of his recovery, and he was anxious to start bantering with his friend again.

"Oh no!" Shawn cried. "It was so nice and quiet when you couldn't talk. Now I'm going to have to put up with all your whining again."

Shawn touched Alvaro's hand. Alvaro squeezed.

The nurses were eager for Alvaro's parents to arrive. Like Shawn, Daisy and Alvaro had no idea that their son was talking. Visiting hours began at 12:30 P.M. At 12:35 the Llanoses walked into the burn unit. Shawn and Melissa Kapner, a burn therapist, had cooked up a plan. Alvaro, who was still wrapped in layers of gauze, with only part of his face and his toes exposed, was out of bed and seated in a chair. He could see only shadows through the slits in his stitched eyelids, so Shawn promised to warn him when his parents were approaching.

"They're coming," he cried in a hushed voice when he saw Daisy and Alvaro senior coming down the hall.

With the Llanoses at the threshold of the room, Melissa leaned over and whispered to Alvaro, who nodded slightly.

When Daisy and Alvaro senior saw their son, they rushed to him. It was the first time he had been out of bed, and they hovered over him, kissing his cheeks and his hands, thanking God for their good fortune. Their boy was out of bed and sitting in a chair. *La gloria a Dios.* Glory to God.

Shawn, leaning against the doorway, his arms crossed over his chest, watched and waited. Pangs of excitement pricked the back of his neck. He saw Melissa pat Alvaro's knee. Showtime.

"Hi, Mommy," Alvaro said, his voice soft but clear. "Hi, Pápi."

Alvaro senior dropped his cane and fell to his knees. He draped himself over his son's lap. "My son!" he cried. "Oh! My son."

Daisy stood there, dazed. How long had she waited to hear her son's voice? How many prayers had she said, asking to be able to hear him say *Mommy* again? How many nights had she gotten on her knees and begged to be able to tell him she loved him and to hear him say, *I love you, too, Mommy,* even if it was just one more time, so she could cherish it in her memory forever?

Daisy felt the deepest joy she had ever known. More even than when she had given birth to her only son, which she didn't mind telling people had been the happiest day of her life. She felt as if a splendid sun was bathing her in warmth, soothing her from the outside in. She smiled a joyous, deeply felt smile.

"He is better," she said softly. "He is really better."

Nurse Majestic stood in the doorway, watching the celebration. She had been there for every one of the small victories. The first nod, when Alvaro acknowledged hearing her voice. The first time he moved a finger, then an arm. His first words. *Hello. Hello. Hello.* She had shared the family's joy with every step forward, and she knew the hardest part of the journey lay ahead. Phase one of the treatment, when the staff did nearly everything to keep the patient alive, was ending. Now it was up to Alvaro to lead the way forward. But for the moment, this was enough.

Within days of being released from the respirator, Alvaro was begging for water. Three months had gone by without a drop of water passing his parched lips. "Water!" he cried, with the desperation of a man stranded in the desert. "I want water." He wasn't allowed to have it. A cardinal rule in the burn intensive care unit was that patients were only allowed sustenance packed with calories. He couldn't afford to waste his appetite on water. He needed milk shakes and ice cream to hasten his healing. Human nature being what it is, because water was forbidden, Alvaro craved it even more, especially now that he was no longer hooked to a breathing machine. All burn patients did. The staff had seen people pull the bags off their IV poles to try to get to the saline inside. They had seen them under sinks, trying to lick the condensation off the pipes. They had seen them trying to gulp the water sprayed from the hoses in the tank room.

"I'm sorry, but you can't have water," Hani explained.

So Alvaro settled on Cherry Coke Slurpees, sucking down as many as were brought to him. The nurses marveled at Alvaro's appetite, and they couldn't believe his sunny disposition. When he didn't have a straw in his mouth, he engaged them with his charm and his wit.

Alvaro remembered only one thing from his long, deep sleep: being taken to the tank room to have his burns scraped and scrubbed. He had hated it when he heard the multitude of quick footsteps and garbled voices approaching in the morning, because he knew it meant he was going somewhere to be tortured.

"I heard you were causing a ruckus in the unit today," one of the tank-room nurses kidded as she prepared to take him for his morning debridement.

"Me?" Alvaro asked, managing to make his weak, slow voice sound incredulous. "You're . . . the . . . one . . . who . . . causes . . . a . . . ruckus."

"Oh yeah? Well, I heard you were banging pots and hollering and causing all kinds of trouble."

"Must . . . have . . . been . . . a . . . ghost," he said.

"Okay, hot shot," another nurse said. "You think you're so smart. Let's see if you remember my name. What is it?"

"Superwoman," Alvaro shot back without skipping a beat.

From the photographs on the wall—which was all there was to go on for months—the nurses had assumed Alvaro was macho and tough. The boy in the pictures looked at the camera with a cocky expression, a look that said, *I'm hot and I know it.* They hadn't expected the sweet, funny kid who emerged from the coma.

They didn't yet know the Alvaro who lay awake at night, worrying and remembering.

Chapter 19

Do you know how long you were asleep?" Daisy asked Alvaro one morning as she rubbed lotion on his bare, leathery hands.

"Yes," Alvaro said. "Three months. One of the nurses told me."

Steeling herself, Daisy pursed her lips and sputtered the question everyone wondered about but didn't want to ask.

"What . . . do you remember about the fire?"

"Everything," Alvaro said without hesitation. "I remember everything."

The answer had surprised Daisy, surprised even the doctors when they heard. After all that Alvaro had been through—running for his life, his whole body on fire, the racking pain of his devastating burns, the morphine-induced coma—no one had expected him to remember much about what had happened that January morning in Boland Hall. The memories of burn patients were often blunted by amnesia, the doctors had explained to Daisy and Alvaro senior; it was the brain's way of protecting them from the psychological trauma of a terrifying event.

Mansour had suspected that if Alvaro remembered the fire at all, his recollection was likely to be scant and confused. It wasn't so. The fire played out in Alvaro's head like a motion picture rewinding itself, time and time again. Sometimes, when he was alone at night, unable to sleep, he closed his eyes and the tragedy cinematically replayed, not a single terrifying detail omitted.

There he was, walking Angie to her room at three in the morning, then e-mailing her good night when he returned to his room, something they always did. He had fallen asleep quickly that night, into a deep sleep, which had been usual for him before the fire. He remembered Shawn waking him because the fire alarm was ringing. At first he was annoyed because he was sure it was another false alarm, Alvaro told Daisy, but Shawn had kept at him—*C'mon, Alvaro. You have to get up, Al*—until he finally got out of bed. He remembered Shawn opening the dorm room door, and the feeling of sheer terror at seeing the blinding, black smoke surging through the hallway. He followed Shawn out, then lost his roommate instantly in the darkness.

Then he had been on his hands and knees, Alvaro recalled, disoriented, frightened, and suffocating in the smoke. *I have to get out,* he remembered telling himself. *I'm not going to die here.* The heat was so searing that at one point he hesitated, not sure whether to turn back and try to find his room again. He couldn't see his hand in front of him. Panicked, he decided to go ahead and crawl toward the stairs near the student lounge on his floor. Just as he did, his clothes caught fire, and flames quickly engulfed his torso. He could feel his back being incinerated, see his clothes burning off his body and falling away.

He had stood up to run — it was instinct, just wanting to get away as quickly as he could — but the flames intensified. Everything started to blur, and his vision narrowed to the size of a pinpoint. He knew that if he fainted he would burn up, so he willed himself forward. It took everything he had to take one step and then another. As he did, he recognized the stairway leading down. He was on fire, stumbling down the stairs, when suddenly a boy and a girl seemed to just appear. He didn't know where they had come from. Maybe he was already dead, he thought, and the boy and girl were angels who had come to rescue him from hell. The angels began beating him with their jackets, the boy screaming at him, *Run! Run!*

Doing as he was told, he had lurched and then tumbled down the rest of the stairs to the main floor of the dormitory. As he did, he could hear Angie's voice calling his name. *Alvaro. Where are you? Al!* The first floor was clear of smoke and he could see students staring at him as he ran, ran as fast as he could, toward the front doors. Through the blur of his delirium, he could still make out the expressions of horror on their faces. He had made it to the main lobby, but finally he couldn't take another step and dropped onto a couch. Every inch of his body hurt, and he was so cold. He sat there, shivering, studying his hands and arms. His skin, he had noticed, was bubbling and shedding off in sheets. A group of students had surrounded him, saying, *Don't worry* and *Everything will be fine.* He thought he was probably okay and took a second to thank God that he wasn't more seriously injured. As he sat on the couch, trying to make sense of what had happened, a girl who identified herself as a nursing student put an oxygen mask over his mouth. Someone else removed the gold chain that hung on his chest. It was red hot and had begun to melt into his neck.

Alvaro paused and took a deep breath.

"Then what happened?" Daisy asked, holding his hand.

"The last thing I remember is being put on a stretcher and carried outside toward an ambulance," Alvaro recalled. Everyone had moved away as he passed by.

"I was worried that you and Pápi wouldn't know where they took me," Alvaro said. "And I was thinking about Angie and Shawn. I wanted to go back in the dorm to make sure they were okay."

Daisy used the palm of her hand to wipe away her tears. Then, taking a tissue from a box at Alvaro's bedside, she wiped away his tears, too.

"How did this happen, Mommy?" Alvaro cried. "Why did it happen?"

"Solamente Dios sabe," Daisy said. *Only God knows.*

There would come a time, and very soon, when Alvaro would want to know more about the fire. Then it would be up to Shawn to tell him what no one else had wanted to: that three students had died that morning in Boland Hall, one of them Alvaro's friend.

Solamente Dios sabe.

In fact, Alvaro wasn't the only one looking for answers. Investigators were working overtime to try to make sure that the truth about what had happened did not become yet another casualty of the blaze. They had their work cut out for them.

Chapter 20

In the story of *Harry Potter and the Sorcerer's Stone,* there is a tall mirror. "A magnificent mirror, as high as the ceiling, with an ornate gold frame, standing on two clawed feet," the story goes. It is called the Mirror of Erised. An inscription carved in an arc around the top reads, "*Erised stra ehru oyt ube cafru oyt on wohsi.*" Read backward, it says, "I show not your face but your heart's desire."

"I dreamed about Alvaro last night, and in my dream he was looking in that mirror," Denise Pinney told her colleagues in the burn ICU one morning. "And in my dream, when he looked in the mirror, he was whole again."

Alvaro would look at himself for the first time in an ordinary handheld mirror. He yearned to see a familiar face when he peered at himself in the glass, but he suspected it was not to be.

Only two weeks earlier, he had asked his mother if his

looks had changed. If he looked like the other burned people he had seen. There were no mirrors in the burn unit except for one on the wall in the nurses' lavatory and one in a drawer at the nurses' station. There was a reason for that. The staff wanted control over when a burn patient saw himself, and they wanted to be there to offer support when it happened.

Alvaro was too afraid to ask the nurses how he looked. It had taken all of his nerve to ask his mother, and he was terrified of the answer. Once, he had tried to steal a glimpse of himself in a stainless-steel paper towel holder in the tank room, but his image was a blur through his partially stitched eyes.

"Is my face burned?" Alvaro had asked that afternoon, when he and Daisy were alone in his room.

Daisy had been dreading the question. She worried that if her son knew he was so badly disfigured, he wouldn't want to live. He would give up after he had come all this way. Mansour had told Daisy right from the start that Alvaro would never be the flawlessly handsome boy he had once been. His appearance had been forever altered by the fire, and no matter how much reconstructive surgery he had, he would always look burned.

That didn't mean Alvaro couldn't live a productive life, the doctor said. He seemed like a boy of great character, the kind of person who could look inside himself and use his own inner strength to build a future. Yes, Daisy had said, that was Alvaro. Beautiful inside and out. That's what everyone had always said: "Oh, Daisy, what a wonderful, beautiful boy you have." There wasn't anyone who compared with Alvaro.

As much as Daisy adored her son, though, as much as she loved the person he was, she was having a difficult time accepting the way he looked. His good looks had been destroyed by the heat and the flames in the dormitory that morning, and as thankful—so very thankful—as she was that he'd survived, she was still anxious about how people, especially strangers, would react to him.

Alvaro's ears had been partially burned off, and his once smooth, brown skin looked like melted wax. The scarring had already distorted his facial features, and the doctors said that would actually get worse as his burns continued to heal and his skin pulled tighter.

How could she expect Alvaro to accept the way he looked when even she was having trouble handling it? Daisy was ashamed of that, but it was the truth.

And so she hedged when Alvaro asked about his face. And then she lied.

"Only your eyelids were burned," she said. "They will get better."

"What other parts of my body were burned?" Alvaro asked, his voice shaking and filled with uncertainty.

Daisy took a deep breath. "Your arms, your back, your chest, and your neck. But don't worry—plastic surgery will take care of everything, and you will be as good as new."

"Okay," Alvaro said, hardly convinced that his mother was telling him the truth.

When the physical therapy team heard about the conversation, they were beside themselves. Of course, Daisy had the best intentions, but lying was the worst thing she could have done. A cardinal rule of the burn unit was never to lie to a patient. The sooner burn victims were told the truth, the faster they were able to deal with the loss of their former selves and work toward accepting their healed but greatly altered bodies.

"This is our fault," Catherine Ruiz, head of occupational therapy, fumed. "Alvaro should have seen himself already. Why hasn't he seen his face yet?"

Melissa Kapner, Alvaro's primary therapist, knew they had failed Alvaro.

"I guess we were sort of putting it off," she said.

Ruiz was certain that Alvaro basically knew the truth. She was just as sure that he was silently torturing himself with anxiety about how he looked.

"Get the mirror," she said to Kapner, a relative newcomer on the staff. "He needs to see his face."

"Right now? . . . Right *now?*"

The most seasoned members of the burn team squirmed when it was time for the mirror to come out. This was Kapner's first time, and the anticipation made her feel nauseated. Alvaro was one of the sweetest young men she had ever met. She wanted to protect him, but she knew that hiding him from himself wasn't the way to do it.

Kapner went to the drawer and pulled out the mirror. It was gray plastic with a long handle, the kind found in any discount drugstore. It was much too ordinary for the task at hand, Kapner thought. She rubbed her hand over its smooth, flat surface and hesitated before heading to Alvaro's room.

When she finally walked through the door, she found Alvaro sitting in a chair by his bed. He smiled when he saw her. She smiled back, then held up the mirror and slowly sat down on the corner of the bed, opposite him.

"It's time for you to see yourself," she said in a voice so gentle that Alvaro could hardly hear her.

"What?"

"It's time for you to look at yourself."

Alvaro's eyes widened. "I don't know," he said. "I'm scared."

"Of course you're scared, sweetie," Kapner said, wishing she were someplace else. "I'm scared, too. But you have to do this. Look, we're all friends here. You can scream. You can cry. We'll be here for you. You have to do this, Al."

Tears streamed down Alvaro's red, leathery cheeks. It had only been the night before that he had lain awake, lamenting how the students at Seton Hall would stare at him, at the new, burned Alvaro Llanos. When the doctor had removed the stitches from his eyes a couple of days earlier, he had seen his hands for the first time, when the nurse changed the dressings, and he hadn't slept much since. These hands didn't look like his hands—they were mottled and bumpy and scary looking. When he studied them, he broke down and cried.

Al had been happy after his hands had been bandaged up again. He thought maybe he would wear gloves for the rest of his life so that no one else would see what his hands looked like. But he couldn't very well hide his face, could he?

Alvaro's thoughts were interrupted by a knock at the door. He looked up and saw Shawn standing there. He was smiling.

"You didn't think I was going to miss this, did you?" Shawn asked, walking to Alvaro's side.

Shawn had been downstairs in occupational therapy. One of the therapists had told him what was happening. He had excused himself, saying he was sorry, he would be back later to stretch his hands, but right now he needed to be with his friend.

Shawn sat on the arm of the chair.

"I'm glad you're here," Alvaro said, looking up at Shawn.

Kapner placed the mirror on Alvaro's lap. He refused to look at it, looking instead at Shawn, who had tears in his eyes.

"C'mon, Al," Shawn said, gently prodding his roommate. "We're in this together, remember? I'm here for you. It's time."

"Al, pick up the mirror," Kapner said gently. "You have to pick it up and look at yourself."

Alvaro took a long, deep breath. Holding on to Shawn's arm with his left hand, he reached for the mirror with his right. Shawn could see his friend was trembling.

Slowly, Alvaro drew the mirror to his face. He stared at his image for a long moment. At first he said nothing as he studied his eyes, then his cheeks, then his chin.

"What's that?" he asked finally, pointing to a dark patch of skin below his mouth.

"Your chin has been grafted," Kapner said. "Your cheeks were not. You still have beautiful eyes, and a beautiful mouth."

Alvaro looked back into the mirror and seemed to freeze. Shawn squeezed his friend's hand as Kapner groped for her next words. The tension in the room was suffocatingly thick. Shawn thought he might be sick.

"Shawn is going through the same thing," Kapner said, but Alvaro seemed not to hear. He just continued to stare into the mirror.

"Al," she said. "Al, look at Shawn's face."

Kapner motioned to Shawn. He pulled off the surgical mask that covered his face from the bottom of his eyes to his chin. The mask was required in the burn ICU, and every time Shawn had visited Alvaro, his face had been covered. Now, for the first time, he took the mask off, revealing his own burned face to his roommate.

Alvaro looked from the mirror to Shawn.

"See, Al," Shawn said pleadingly. "I look like you. I told you, we're going to get through this together."

Alvaro silently studied Shawn's face. The moment seemed more like an hour to Shawn. Then Alvaro looked into the mirror one last time. He wouldn't tell anyone what he saw, but it wasn't anything like the face he had grown up with. It wasn't the face of the boy his parents had been so proud to introduce, and it wasn't the face of the person Angie had fallen in love with.

This isn't my face, Alvaro thought as he stared at himself. *This isn't me. I hate this face.*

"Okay," Alvaro said finally, his voice filled with resignation. He put the mirror down on his lap. A sense of revulsion rolled through his entire body. *I'm so ugly,* he thought. *What am I going to do?*

Chapter 21

Two days after Alvaro saw himself in the mirror, Shawn asked Catherine Ruiz if patients ever wore gloves after their burns had healed. "Sometimes," Catherine said. "But we don't recommend it. The sooner you get used to your scars, the faster you'll be able to get on with your life."

Used to his scars? Shawn wasn't convinced that would ever happen. He was pretty sure it wouldn't. "I think I will keep wearing them," he said. "Maybe I'll wear them forever." Despite Mansour's initial predictions that Shawn would lose his fingers, early grafting with skin from his thighs had saved his hands, but to Shawn they still looked like melted wax and they were deeply embarrassing to him. What made matters worse was that no one was willing to reassure him that they would ever appear normal again.

Mansour had told Shawn that scarring was unpredictable and he couldn't make promises about how his hands would ultimately look once the scarring and the grafting was done. Genetics played a role, he explained. Dark-skinned people generally scarred more than people with lighter skin, and the darker the skin, the more likely the scars were to be thick and raised, which was bad news for Shawn.

The scarring process went on for one to two years, Hani had told Shawn, so it was common for burn patients to look worse when they were fully healed than when they first left the burn unit. That had frightened Shawn more than anything else the doctor said. Every morning he studied his image in the bathroom mirror, looking for changes. Each new bump and blemish caused him alarm. *Look at this, Mom,* he would say, calling Christine to the mirror. *What is that?* Studying his face, Shawn wondered whether the rich brown color would ever return to his now pink, mottled cheeks. And would his hair grow back thick and curly, the way it had been before the fire?

Sometimes, Shawn didn't help himself. The doctors didn't know if it was stubbornness or depression, but he rarely wore the clear plastic mask prescribed for him—even though they had told him the mask could significantly reduce his facial disfigurement by stretching the skin and compressing the scars. The scarring process was aggressive and constant—twenty-four hours a day. "You can't let it get ahead of you," Mansour had explained.

Catherine scolded Shawn when he didn't wear his mask.

"The more hours you are out of it, the scar will grow thick and bumpy and can distort your features," she told

Shawn. "Do you understand?" Shawn understood very well. But the mask was tight and hot. When he wore it, he felt as if he were suffocating and looked like the killer in the horror movie *Halloween*. So, stubbornly, he decided he would rather deal with some disfigurement than have to wear the damn mask for twelve hours a day.

What he couldn't deal with were his hands. They were so hideous looking that he rarely removed his tight-fitting black Jobst gloves, prescribed to compress his scarring. When he occasionally misplaced one, he became agitated and shoved his hands into his pockets. Shawn knew the gloves stopped working when the scarring process was finished. *What then?* he wondered.

"I know my mother and a lot of my women friends have said they always look at a man's hands first, and I always kept my hands nice," Shawn told a friend. "Catherine says she knows people who continue wearing the gloves after the healing process is done. Maybe I'll have some nice custom leather gloves made."

At least his girlfriend wasn't bothered by his burns, Shawn said. Shawn had met Tiha in music class at University High in Newark. They had become fast friends and had started dating a year later. The fire had made them closer than ever. "Tiha doesn't care about my burns at all," Shawn said. "I could never, ever see her leaving me because of my burns. I'm more concerned about strangers' reactions."

Shawn had come a long way in the months since he had left Saint Barnabas, and he was making significant gains in his daily ninety-minute outpatient sessions with Ruiz. The third-degree burns had caused a loss of sensation in Shawn's hands, but the exercises with Catherine had begun to give him back some of the flexibility and strength he lost as the scars tightened his skin, constricting his hand movement. He could dress himself again, except for buttons. He was also able to bathe himself, wash his own hair, and brush his own teeth. He could pull on his gloves and turn a doorknob with one hand. Catherine anticipated that Shawn could eventually regain 90 percent of the dexterity in his hands—but there was no guarantee, even with additional surgery or skin grafts, which he resisted. Chronic pain in his joints and from his scars sometimes caused Shawn to wince when Catherine bent and stretched his hands. The corners of Shawn's mouth were so tight from scarring that he could open it only half as wide as before he was burned. Even laughing was hard. Shawn wanted more than anything else to drive again, but that was still weeks away.

Even when impatient, Shawn impressed. "He'll kick and bite and scream, but he'll get better anyway," Catherine predicted in a team meeting in mid-April. "For an eighteen-year-old, he has the capacity to handle so much. He has such inner strength. He has a level of faith that most people don't. A lot of this comes from his mother, and he's extremely lucky to have her.

"The way people deal with burns is the same as the grieving process," Catherine added. "You're grieving the body image you had prior to the burn. Burn patients mourn their looks years later. Anger, denial, sadness, acceptance—that's what I expect burn patients to go through. Right now I see all four of them in Shawn. I see him angry, but I also see him planning ahead, and that is acceptance."

Alvaro had his eye on the future, too. His burns were bleeding less, so he no longer required twice-daily blood transfusions. (Since the fire, the blood in his body had been replaced six times.) The doctors had told him it would be at least a year, and probably much longer, before he was fully healed. In the burn unit, that meant simply that his burns no longer oozed and were sufficiently covered by either scars or skin grafts to resist infection. Reconstructive surgeries on his torso, arms, hands, face, and neck would prolong the process, Mansour explained. Alvaro was eighteen years old. He would probably be in his midtwenties before everything that could be done was done, the doctor said.

Alvaro was eager to get on with it. His daily routine at Saint Barnabas was heavy and exhausting. There was physical therapy to restore his agility and build his strength and endurance. And there was occupational therapy to relearn the basics, such as walking, writing, and feeding himself. Every step Alvaro took was hailed as a victory, his first ten steps earning him a round of applause from the burn staff, his first twenty-five, a standing ovation. Pushing a video into the VCR, raising a fork to his mouth, holding a cup of juice, were all causes for joy.

The toughest part of recovery was also the most critical: stretching his burned skin to counteract the scarring. That job fell to Roy Bond. For an hour every morning, the strapping physical therapist bent, pushed, and pulled the boy's grafted arms. Then he kneaded the thickening scar tissue from Alvaro's chin to his neck until Alvaro screamed in pain. Sometimes the scarred skin would rip from the stretching and spurt blood.

"It's a constant tug-of-war between you and the scar," Bond said one day when Alvaro begged him to stop. "You can't say, *Okay, I'll do this tomorrow,* because the scar will win."

The problem of scarring was much more than cosmetic, Bond explained as tears gushed from Alvaro's eyes. Scars could cause muscles and joints to contract permanently, leading to deformities. Without the rigorous therapy, Alvaro could wind up unable to raise his arms, or even to move his head from side to side.

"Is that what you want?" Bond asked gently. "You won't be able to open a cabinet, or drive your car, or hug Angie."

For a boy whose future seemed so far off, Alvaro had big plans. He had told Bond he wanted to finish school, find a good job, buy a house for his parents, and one day marry Angie and have a family, a boy and a girl.

"What about your plans?" Bond asked. "What about your dreams?"

"Give me more," Alvaro said, crying harder.

"That's my boy," Bond said, obeying the order.

Placing his huge hands on Alvaro's maimed chest, Bond pressed and squeezed the ravaged skin. Alvaro grimaced and bit his lip so hard it bled.

"Go on, Roy!" he screamed. "Keep stretching! I don't want to be deformed. I want to be the old Alvaro. I want to get out of here and go home."

Wednesday, May 10, started out happily. When Alvaro arrived downstairs for his morning physical therapy session, he found the room dressed for a party. Colored ribbons streamed from the walls, and a piñata shaped like a baseball dangled from the ceiling. Shawn appeared, leading a rousing chorus of "Happy Birthday," and all of the therapists and patients stopped what they were doing and joined in. When the singing stopped, Shawn handed Alvaro a baseball bat and told him to "have at" the piñata. Seated in his wheelchair, the now nineteen-year-old Alvaro took the bat and slowly brought it back behind his head, then, with all his might, swung at the piñata. The papier-mâché baseball burst open, and candy rained over the therapy room as everyone whooped and clapped. It was his first time swinging a bat since the fire.

He decided to make it a day of firsts.

"Let's see if I can write," Alvaro said, looking at Shawn as the others swept up the candy. Shawn fetched a pen, and the therapists provided a clipboard with paper. Shawn put the clipboard on Alvaro's lap and held out the pen. Alvaro took the pen and gripped it in his gloved right hand. It shook so violently that he had to steady it with his left. Both hands, one supporting the other, paused for a moment over the paper. Then Alvaro began to write. The message took a few moments to compose. The writing was small and shaky, but the feeling was clear.

"Shawn You Are a Good Friend."

From the moment Shawn and Alvaro had met, nine months earlier, at the start of their freshman year, their relationship had been based on joking and kidding each other. Shawn needled Alvaro about being neat like a girl. Alvaro cracked about Shawn's clothes always being strewn around the dorm room. Shawn teased Alvaro about being bookish. Alvaro chided Shawn about having so many girlfriends that he couldn't keep their names straight. So Shawn had not expected such tenderness from his roommate, and the sentiment moved him.

"Oh my goodness, Alvaro," he said, looking at his friend's heartfelt words. Shawn laughed at first, half-embarrassed, and then he choked up. "I thought you were going to write something silly."

Alvaro just smiled.

An hour later, back upstairs in the burn unit, the birthday celebration continued. As Shawn wheeled Alvaro to his room, the nurses gathered around them. "This way," one of them said, directing the boys to the second-floor nurses' lounge. On a table was a birthday cake with maple-walnut icing and the words "Happy Birthday Alvaro" written on it.

Next to it sat a gift box with purple ribbon wrapped around it and a matching bow on top. Shawn opened it for Alvaro. Inside was a music box. Inscribed on the top was "A friend is one who knows you as you are, understands where you've been, accepts who you've become." Alvaro looked at the box for a long time. His lip quivered as if he were about to cry. He looked at each of the nurses. All were in tears. The nurses accepted him for who he had become. And Shawn did, too. But what about everyone else? Alvaro wondered. What about strangers on the street? And the girls who used to flirt with him? What about his classmates back at Seton Hall? Would they accept him the way he was now? All Alvaro could say was, "Thank you." *Thank you for accepting me for who I have become.*

At five o'clock, Angie arrived in Alvaro's room, and she and Shawn and Alvaro talked and laughed like old times. They talked about safe things—movies and music videos, that sort of stuff. Daisy and Alvaro senior sat in the corner, leafing through magazines, barely acknowledging Angie's presence. They had spent the afternoon preparing for a family birthday party that was to take place later in the day, and they hadn't expected to see Angie at the hospital. She had been coming less and less. The tension between Angie and Alvaro's family had been simmering for weeks, ever since Angie went away for spring break. It was about to boil over.

Feeling as if she could no longer be in the same room with Angie, Daisy abruptly rose from her chair and walked to the visitors' lounge down the hall. She had bit her lip to stop herself from saying something that would hurt her son. Now she complained bitterly to one of the nurses. Angie hadn't brought her son a birthday present, Daisy noted. She hadn't even wished him a happy birthday. How could she be so thoughtless?

"I used to love her. No more," Daisy said, her voice sharp with bitterness. "She doesn't love my son."

The nurse tried to make Daisy see things differently. Angie was just a teenager, she said. Adults didn't react well when their loved ones were burned. "She's just a kid. Don't expect too much of her." But Daisy didn't want to hear it.

"I don't want her here," she said. "I want her to leave."

"What does Alvaro want?" the nurse asked.

"My son still loves her," Daisy admitted. "I know he does. I see it in his eyes."

The second birthday party got under way at dinnertime. In bunches, Alvaro's extended family arrived in the waiting room and chattered excitedly in Spanish until the guest of honor was due to arrive. The tiny area, just outside the burn unit, was jammed with aunts, uncles, cousins, and friends. Contemporary Latin music played softly in the background from a radio someone had brought, and a giant buttercream sheet cake waited to be cut.

When Shawn pushed Alvaro, in his wheelchair, into the middle of the crowd, a roar of well-wishing greeted him. Everyone took turns having his photo taken with the birthday boy. But Alvaro's sisters, ever protective of their only brother, edged Angie out as she approached to have her picture taken with him.

Crowded out and ignored by everyone but Shawn, Angie retreated to a corner and stood by herself, pretending to watch an old episode of *Bewitched* on the TV suspended from the ceiling. While everyone else laughed and danced, she folded her arms across her chest and stared at the screen. Trying not to let anyone see as her eyes misted over, she thought about the year before, when she had planned the party for Alvaro and even made the birthday cake herself. Shawn came to her side and held her hand.

Angie felt the tears seeping from the outer corners of her eyes. Determined not to let Alvaro's family see her cry, she pushed her way through the crowd of relatives, people who had once welcomed her but now looked at her with expressions of disdain and disgust. She got to Alvaro just as the candles on his cake were lit.

Leaning in close so that no one could hear her but him, Angie said, "I love you. I really love you."

Alvaro couldn't look at her. "I know you're leaving," he said.

"Your family doesn't want me here. You see that, right?"

Alvaro wouldn't take sides. How could he? Without Angie, his family was all he had. He wasn't about to alienate them. He needed them, and they loved him.

"I want you here, but I know you have to leave," he said, still looking past her.

The candles began to melt into the cake while the two dozen family members and friends waited awkwardly. Angie kissed Alvaro on the cheek. Then she pushed her way back through the crowd toward the elevator at the end of the hall. The doors parted and she rushed in, sobbing into her hands. Shawn reached the elevator just as the doors smacked shut. Angie was gone.

"Blow out the candles!" Alvaro's family cried, and Alvaro obeyed. As his sisters cut the cake, Alvaro cried, too. He had wanted more than anything else to spend his birthday with Angie, and now she was gone.

He wondered if she would ever come back.

Chapter 22

Alvaro was crying. His stomach ached and his head throbbed. Lunch was meat loaf. He hated meat loaf.

"What can we do for you?" the kindly woman asked, looking at his untouched meal.

"Nothing," Alvaro said, choking out the word. "I just want to be left alone."

A week earlier, the nurses in the burn unit had been serenading him with "Happy Birthday." Now he was in a strange place, in a strange room, with people he didn't know, and he was miserable.

"The physical therapist will be in to see you soon, honey," the woman said, handing Alvaro a tissue. "You're scheduled for the gym this afternoon."

"I want to be left alone!" Alvaro cried, wiping his tears.

Alvaro had arrived at the Kessler Institute for Rehabilitation a few hours earlier. He hadn't been there a full day, and already he was expected to go to the gymnasium for physical therapy? He had no intention of leaving his room. Not yet. No way.

Kessler, located in nearby West Orange, was reputed to be one of the finest rehabilitation centers in the country. The nurse who had escorted Alvaro from the ambulance to his room that morning had pointed proudly to the arena-sized gym and explained that five years earlier, Christopher Reeve, Superman, had trained there after a fall from a horse had rendered him a quadriplegic. The center was ranked one of the top two in the country by a survey of physicians published in *U.S. News & World Report,* and the best facility of its kind on the East Coast. Patients came from as far away as Europe and Japan, and the waiting list was miles long. Mansour had called in plenty of favors to get Alvaro a spot.

Kessler had been in business for fifty years and was considered a pioneer in physical medicine and rehabilitation, the nurse said. Besides spinal cord injuries, the center treated patients with brain injuries and strokes. Some patients were recovering from car accidents; others, from hip and knee replacements or lost limbs.

The gym looked like a big-city health club to Alvaro, with exercise machines and mats on the floor. He had seen dozens of people in there when he looked in, most of them in wheelchairs. But no one else was burned. Not another scarred body in the place.

The only reason Alvaro had left Saint Barnabas smiling that morning was that it meant he was a step closer to home. He wanted more than anything to be back in Paterson with his parents and sisters. Now he thought about what he had left behind. The people in the burn unit had saved his life, and they had become family. More important, he had felt safe with them. They had seen him scream. Seen him cry. Seen his burned body naked and not even winced. How would people here react when they saw him?

Sitting on his new bed, Alvaro conjured up the memory of Sue Manzo bringing him a water gun so that he could soak the rest of the staff, then arguing with the doctors that he should be able to keep it because it was good therapy for his hands. His thoughts drifted to Ann Marie Majestic, who had sat and talked baseball with him for hours after her shift ended, when she could have gone home to be with her family. Andy Horvath had been the only nurse who could soothe him during the tortured hours in the tank room, when his raw burns were scraped until they bled. Sometimes what happened in that tank room was so agonizing that the nurses cried with him, and those were the times Andy would lean in close to his face and whisper that everything would be all right, and just because of the way he said it, Alvaro believed him.

Now there was no Sue Manzo, no Ann Marie Majestic, no Andy Horvath to turn to, and Alvaro didn't know what to do.

That morning, a cool, sunny Tuesday in late May, the whole staff had gathered around as Alvaro prepared to leave the burn unit for Kessler. As they crowded into his room, everyone had shed tears. Tears of sadness. Tears of gratitude. Tears of pride. Tears, too, because the nurses knew there were many hardships ahead for Alvaro. You could survive cancer and heart disease. Mend broken bones. But burns never went away.

Alvaro had been helped into a wheelchair and was about to be wheeled downstairs to the ambulance waiting outside, when Roy Bond rushed into his room. Alvaro smiled.

"I feel like I'm sending my son off to war," the husky therapist said, biting his lip. "I love you, man."

Alvaro looked at Bond and thought he might like to stay in the burn unit for the rest of his life. If he stayed there, he would never have to worry about people staring at him, or ostracizing him, or feeling sorry for him. But then he remembered what Eileen Gehringer, one of his nurses, had told him: "It hurts to see you go, but you are on to better things." Better things like college classes and movies with friends and driving his car, all the things a regular teenager did. How he wanted to get back to being a regular kid again and not having to worry about stained bandages under his clothing, or waking up on bloody sheets, or hand tremors, or relentless fatigue, or taking a dozen pills a day—pills for pain, pills for depression, pills for anxiety, pills for itching, pills to sleep. He just wanted to play baseball and hang out with his cousins and kiss Angie.

A week earlier, after his birthday party in the burn unit, Alvaro had said to Bond, "In the beginning, when this first happened, I used to think, *Why me?* But I don't do that much anymore. In the beginning I was scared that when I went back to school, people would be staring. Now I'm getting comfortable with who I am. It's like I've been reborn, like I'm starting life all over again." Now, at Kessler, where he didn't know anyone, and no one knew him, his resolve was cracking. His untouched lunch had grown cold. Pushing aside the meat loaf, Alvaro turned up the volume on the TV, crawled under the covers, and muffled his sobs with his pillow.

"Hello there!" The athletic-looking woman with the ponytail and pink button-down sweater strode into Alvaro's room with a grin on her face and a clipboard under her arm. "We've been waiting for you for-*eh*-vuh," she said, her accent giving away her Long Island childhood. "I assume you are the famous Alvaro! It's so great to meet you. You're already a rock star around here, you know. We've heard so much about you. I'm so happy you're here."

Alvaro looked up from his bed. His eyes hurt from crying so much, and hunger growled deep in his belly because he hadn't eaten since first thing that morning, before he left Saint Barnabas, yet he couldn't help smiling at the woman standing over him. She was pretty, he thought, and bubbly, as bubbly as Angie.

"I'm Dr. Benevento," she said, "and I'll be in charge of your medical team here. We have some work to do."

"You're my doctor?" Alvaro asked.

"'Fraid so," she said, her grin growing into a full-blown smile.

Barbara Benevento had been treating patients at Kessler for three years. She was thirty-nine, single, and a favorite with the patients. She liked to say she had no life outside of her job, except for once-yearly adventures in some faraway place, which this year was to be an African safari, if all things went as planned, and they rarely did.

A physiatrist, or doctor of physical medicine, Benevento specialized in spinal cord injuries, and she had quickly made a reputation for herself at Kessler. Burns were new to Benevento, and she had spent hours on the telephone with Mansour in the preceding weeks, mapping out Alvaro's treatment plan. What she didn't know about burns, though, she knew about boys, having grown up the only girl in a family of four brothers. When word had reached her that her newest patient was resisting a trip to the gym and refusing to eat, she had headed straight for his room with a game plan.

"What's up with the meat loaf?" she asked, glancing down at the shriveled slab of meat on Alvaro's tray. It had sat there for nearly three hours.

"I don't like meat loaf," Alvaro said.

"Me, either," Benevento said, crinkling up her nose. "I'd rather have a hamburger."

"Me, too," Alvaro said.

"I hear you don't feel like going to the gym," Benevento said.

"Yeah. Well, I guess I'm tired and I don't feel good."

"You worried about meeting new people?"

"Yeah, I guess so."

"You think everyone's going to look at you because you're the new guy in town?"

"No one else is burned," Alvaro said.

"Ah. So you think people are going to look at you because you're burned?"

"Yeah."

"Hmm. Do you trust me, kid?"

"I think so."

"Then try to hear what I'm saying. No one is going to give you a second look. I promise. Everyone in the gym has their own problems. Big problems. They're too busy trying to get better to pay much attention to anything else or anyone else.

"Now, can I tell you a secret?"

Alvaro was gulping down the last of his lunchtime hamburger, compliments of Dr. Benevento, when his parents arrived the following day, his second day at Kessler.

"Guess what I heard," he whispered conspiratorially.

"What?" Daisy and Alvaro senior asked.

"Even Superman didn't go to the gym when he first got here."

"¿De verdad?" his parents cried. *Really?*

"Yes, really!" Alvaro said.

Dr. Benevento had told Alvaro that even though Reeve was at Kessler before she got there, she had learned on good authority that it had taken days for him to get up the courage to leave his room and go to the gym for therapy.

"So don't worry," she had said during their talk the day before. "You'll know when you're ready, just like Superman knew when he was ready. Just remember what I told you. No one will be looking at you, I promise. And the faster we get going, the quicker you'll leave here to go home.

"Oh, and don't tell anyone our little secret."

"So I wasn't supposed to say anything," Alvaro was saying to his mother and father. "But I had to tell you because—"

"Tell what?" asked an athletic-looking young man with a brown crew cut, interrupting the conversation as he marched into Alvaro's room. His name was J. R. Nisivoccia, Alvaro's new physical therapist, and he had popped in the night before, right after Benevento had left, to introduce himself. Alvaro had taken to J. R. right away. He was only eight years older, he didn't flinch or look at Alvaro funny, and he liked to talk baseball.

J. R. sat at the foot of Alvaro's bed.

"Well, my friend," he said, "you've had a day to rest. Do you want to get up and walk around your room, or do you want to hit the hallway?"

Alvaro hesitated, then slowly swung his legs off the bed, placing his feet solidly on the floor.

"Let's hit the hallway," he said, his body weak, but his voice strong and determined.

"That's what we like to see," J. R. said. "A motivated patient."

"We're off," Alvaro said, looking over his shoulder at his parents as he headed out of his room.

Even Superman took longer than that.

While Alvaro settled into a routine at Kessler, Shawn returned to Seton Hall and registered for the fall semester. It was his first time on campus since the fire, five months earlier. The dean of freshmen studies had made special arrangements for him to register privately with her. She had wanted to take her time with him, she had said, to make sure he was getting every advantage and got into every class he chose. Shawn swept past the other students waiting outside the dean's office and walked quickly toward the woman who was seated behind a big cherry desk and waving him inside. A window air conditioner that had seen better days cranked loudly behind her, but the room temperature was still sweltering, and Shawn pushed away streams of perspiration that dripped down the sides of his face. Maybe it wasn't the heat. Maybe he was just excited. Or nervous.

"Hello, Shawn!" the dean said, her mouth forming a big, toothy smile. "It's wonderful to see you. Now let's get started."

Shawn stayed ten minutes and signed up for fifteen credits: three business classes, English, and algebra. He would still be a freshman when he returned to school in the fall, but he was determined to catch up by taking extra courses.

"Will you be living on campus?" the dean asked Shawn, stealing glances at his burned hands as he filled out the necessary forms. Shawn guessed that the dean was around his mother's age, but she seemed nervous and unsure of herself.

"No," Shawn said plaintively.

"I understand," she said. "Is this your first time back on campus?"

No, you don't understand, Shawn thought. "Yeah," he answered.

"Was it tough?"

Nah, it wasn't tough. Three of my classmates died here and I almost died that day, too. My roommate is so badly scarred you wouldn't even know him now, and his lungs are so damaged that he'll never run the bases again. And, oh, I noticed you were looking at my hands. They look like something out of a horror flick, don't they, but . . .

"Uh, no, not really."

"Good, then. You're all set, Shawn. We're glad to have you back."

"Yeah. Glad to be back." *Don't know if I'll stay.*

Shawn rose to leave. He thrust his arm out to shake the woman's hand and noticed that, for just an instant, she hesitated before taking his.

Shawn didn't linger on campus, nor did he mention wanting to see Boland Hall. The dean hadn't offered. She was nice enough, but she seemed relieved when their meeting was over. Shawn thought he understood why. The fire was a stain on Seton Hall. There hadn't been sprinklers in Boland Hall, and the state had taken over fire inspections at the university after finding that the buildings on campus had not been properly inspected for nearly five years. School officials also had seemed insensitive to the students who were injured in the fire. Right after the fire, Monsignor Robert Sheeran had visited the injured students and spent time with their families in the Saint Barnabas waiting room, but the visits had quickly tapered off after a Seton Hall student was appointed liaison to the families and seemed to alienate some of the medical staff and families. Shawn's mother thought the monsignor's visits stopped at the advice of the university's lawyers, and that had made her even madder than if Sheeran himself had decided to stay away. All these months after the fire, no one seemed to know how the fire had started, or who had set it. Sometimes it seemed to Shawn as if school officials wished people would just forget. Meanwhile, he could end up sitting next to the arsonist in class and he wouldn't even know it.

Shawn thought about Alvaro. "Now it's just a matter of time and determination and we'll be back to school together," he said to his mother when he got home that day.

"I think if he decided to go back and stay on campus, I'd ask him to room with me, and I'd go back and live there, too. We've grown so close. It's going to be hard if we decide to do that, but I think we could support each other through it. I just can't handle living here right now without him, knowing he's still struggling to get better."

"I know, baby boy," Christine said. "In time. In time."

Alvaro's first time in the gym at Kessler had been as uneventful as Benevento had promised. No one had stopped what they were doing when he walked in. One or two patients may have glanced sideways at him, but he may have imagined that, too. No one else was scarred, but some were totally paralyzed and some couldn't even speak. The second time was easier, and the third time some of the other patients included him in their conversation. He had been at Kessler six days when he asked that his therapy time be doubled from three hours a day to six. His goals were to increase his upper-body strength using weight machines and to relearn everyday agility tasks: shuffling cards, holding a glass, twisting a cap off a jar.

Mansour had predicted that Alvaro's stay at the rehabilitation center would last two months. Benevento and the rest of the Kessler team agreed it would be at least that long before he could go home. Everyone hoped that would be sometime in late summer or early fall. After that, he still would be faced with at least two years of daily outpatient therapy at Saint Barnabas.

Laps around the gym and playing basketball in the courtyard outside became daily rituals for Alvaro at Kessler. Standing five feet from the hoop, he slowly and deliberately tossed free throws underhand because his scar tissue prevented him from raising his arms above his shoulders. Even walking was still difficult for him. His gait was slow and unsteady and he sometimes lost his balance. Picking up the basketball was hardest of all, and it was the exercise Alvaro hated the most: bending over from the waist. Still, he hardly ever missed a basket. He would lift the ball, step to the free throw line, take a breath, and shoot. It was J. R.'s job to retrieve the balls and to catch Alvaro when he fell.

Bending over was difficult because Alvaro's back had been incinerated in the fire, and the burn surgeons at Saint Barnabas had been forced to cut away layers of burned skin before they found a healthy bed for skin grafts. As a result, even now, parts of his back were still open and oozing blood and fluids. The slightest wrong movement could cause the fragile skin to break and bleed. Sometimes the pain was still so bad that Alvaro screamed after reaching for something, or turning over, or bending from the waist. But whenever he was tempted to slack off or hide in his room again, J. R. would remind Alvaro about his dark blue Mazda Millenia waiting at home, or about the prospect of sleeping in his own bed. Alvaro thought about his mom's home-cooked rice and beans and Sunday afternoons the way they used to be, when all of his cousins gathered at his house to play dominoes or watch the Mets on TV. One day after his parents brought him a lunch of Chinese takeout, Alvaro cracked open his fortune cookie and read aloud: "A handful of patience is worth more than a bushel of brains." He tossed it aside, telling his parents he had more brains than patience. He wanted to go home.

So Alvaro worked harder than anyone in the gym. When J. R. wanted him to do ten repetitions on a weight machine, he did twelve or thirteen. When J. R. told him to walk two laps around the gym, he walked three. When everyone else went to lunch at noon and the gym cleared out, Alvaro stayed, sitting at a table, tightening the cap on an empty peanut butter jar over and over or placing one more building block on a stack. The exercises seemed silly sometimes, but the more he did them, the more limber his scarred hands became and the less they trembled.

"By the time you get out of here, we're going to be calling you Arnold," J. R. said, using his best Schwarzenegger accent.

"Or Superman," Alvaro said, smiling.

It was rare for someone Alvaro's age, with a devastating injury, not to be bitter. Benevento had seen hundreds of desperately sick patients come through Kessler's gym. Many of them were heroic in their efforts to get better, but few were as determined as Alvaro.

"If you hang around long enough, you learn there's something in certain people, an inner strength," Benevento said to an intern one day as they watched Alvaro slowly walking laps, trying to catch his breath, and holding a cane to steady himself if he started to fall. Six months earlier, he had been practicing his swing in anticipation of tryouts for Seton Hall's baseball team.

"They will take the worst disadvantage and turn it into an advantage. He's one of those people. From the first minute you look into his eyes, you know this kid has that inner strength. You can't buy that. This is a kid that, whatever it takes, he's going to do it. He's still a kid, a little boy. If he was any other person, he would be lying in a bed, depressed.

"Every day people ask me, 'Why do you do this? Why do you stay? It must be so depressing.'" She pointed to Alvaro. "That's why."

Chapter 23

A collective gasp rose from the fifth-grade class at Newark's Rafael Hernandez Elementary School when Shawn walked into the classroom.

"It's him," the wide-eyed students cried when they saw Shawn.

"It's Shawn!"

"Hi, Shawn!"

"Wow!"

"Shawn!"

The elementary school was one of dozens around the country that had corresponded with the Seton Hall students burned in the fire. Shawn had received hundreds of letters, most of them from strangers, many from schoolchildren. He had promised to visit the inner-city school in his hometown when he was well enough. So here he was, at the end of June, all dressed up in a pressed shirt and crisp jeans, with a

Yankees baseball cap concealing his burned scalp, and his burned hands buried in tan-colored pressure gloves.

"Good morning," Shawn said, standing at the front of the classroom, like a teacher ready to begin his morning lesson. "I'm really happy to be here, and I understand you have a lot of questions. Who wants to go first?"

Every hand in the room shot up.

"Let's take it one by one. How about you?" Shawn said to a little girl with braided hair, seated in the front row.

"How did the fire start?" the little girl asked.

"Right now, no one is sure if it was an accident or a prank," Shawn answered with the dispassion of a person reciting a shopping list. "Next?" Shawn said.

"Did you run out of the fire?" a boy in a plaid shirt asked excitedly.

"No. You should always get on the floor when you're in a fire. *Always* get on the floor. There's more oxygen there."

"Is it scary not knowing who did it?"

Shawn groped for words. "It's, um . . . it's kind of scary, yes. When I'm in class at Seton Hall, I could be sitting next to the person who did it and I wouldn't even know."

"Do your hands hurt?"

"It hurts when I'm doing therapy. Not right now, here with you."

"Do you have nightmares?"

"No. But most people do. I think about what happened a lot."

"Is your friend still in the hospital?"

"Yes. He's in a different hospital now. He's in a rehabilitation hospital. He was burned worse."

Shawn fielded questions for nearly an hour, laughing at the bluntness of some and answering others as if he were talking not about himself but about an acquaintance.

The fire had been a national news story and it had made Shawn a local celebrity. His picture had been in the newspaper numerous times, and everywhere he went, someone would ask if he was one of the Seton Hall students who were burned in Boland Hall. He had been approached in malls, in gas stations, in restaurants, and on the street. Everyone had a question, and he answered every one. *How are you feeling?* Fine. *Are you going back to school?* Yes. *Back to Seton Hall?* Yes. *Will you live in the dorm?* Not yet. In some ways, Shawn enjoyed his new fame. He had always been outgoing, and easily slipped into the role of being the center of attention. He didn't mind talking to strangers or answering their questions.

Today, though, one question caught him off guard.

"Could you have saved your roommate?" a curly-haired boy with large brown eyes asked.

The room went silent except for the sound of the teacher catching her breath.

Shawn's eyes turned dark. A moment passed. "If I could just go back, I would definitely make him go a different way," he said quietly, more to himself than to the children in the room.

"One more question," the teacher said. "Shawn's tired. He's spent a lot of time with us." A dozen hands in the air.

"You," Shawn said, pointing to a shy-looking girl seated at a desk next to him.

"Are you scared that this will happen again?" she asked so quietly he could hardly hear her.

"No, I'm not worried," Shawn said softly. "I doubt that anything like this will ever happen again."

What Shawn didn't say was that the previous Monday he had awakened in his bedroom, certain that he smelled smoke. It was dark outside. He looked at the clock. Four thirty—the same time he had been awakened by the fire alarms in Boland Hall five months earlier. At first, Shawn froze in his bed. Then he made himself get up and crawl on the floor, his heart pounding, his breath short, out of his room and into his mother's room, where Christine was fast asleep.

"Mom," he cried in a hoarse whisper. "Mom! Wake up! Mom! I smell smoke."

Christine awoke with a start.

"What is it? What is it, Shawn?" she asked, trying to make sense of what was happening.

"I smell fire," Shawn said. "There's a fire."

Christine jumped out of bed and, with Shawn on her heels, went room to room, inspecting the whole apartment. Everything looked normal. She turned to Shawn.

"I don't smell anything," she said gently.

Still, to calm him, she went on to check every electrical outlet and every appliance in the house. She turned the dials on the gas stove to make sure all of them were securely off. She ran downstairs to the basement to check the furnace, and it was cold to the touch. Then, finding nothing inside the house, Christine walked outside and looked up and down Halstead Street, with Shawn watching from the door. There was nothing. Just a sleeping city block a couple of hours before dawn.

"I don't see or smell anything," Christine told Shawn. "There's no fire, Son. Go back to bed now and try to get some sleep."

Not five minutes passed, and Christine felt her boy's presence, then saw his shadow in her bedroom doorway.

"What's up, Shawn?" Christine asked, the ever-patient mother.

"Mom, I have to know where it's coming from," Shawn said, his voice quivering with anxiety.

Christine rose from her bed, pulled on her clothes, and grabbed the car keys from the top of her bureau.

"C'mon, baby boy," she said. "Let's go see what we can find."

For the next half hour, Christine and Shawn drove through the streets of Newark, searching for a fire. It was only after Christine had pulled up to the nearest fire station and Shawn had seen all of the trucks parked inside that he finally agreed to go home to bed.

The plain white envelope arrived with Alvaro's breakfast tray.

"What's this?" he asked Benevento, who had personally delivered his eggs to his room that morning in late June.

"What's what?"

"This."

"Oh. That. Humph. Guess we'll have to open it and see," the doctor said, acting like the cat that swallowed the canary.

Benevento picked up the envelope and plucked a piece of paper from inside. She unfolded it and paused.

"Looks like a day pass," she said, holding up the paper. "It says here you get to leave this wonderful place on Saturday afternoon to go to a Mets game."

Alvaro's eyes widened. "For real?"

"Seems like it's for real."

A day earlier, Alvaro and the doctor had been talking baseball, the Mets, of course—the only team worth talking about, if you asked Alvaro. He had told her he had never been to Shea Stadium, even though he hadn't missed a Mets game on TV, not a single one, since he was a little kid.

"Would you want to go?" she had asked, thinking he probably wasn't anywhere near ready to face a crowd.

"Yeah!" Alvaro had answered without hesitating. The next day the doctor had the tickets in her hand.

Benevento could recite countless stories of bravery she had witnessed at Kessler over the years, but she was awed by her young burn patient's courage. According to the books she'd read on burns, Alvaro was still at the point where he should be hiding under the covers, in the depths of despair, afraid to face the world as a burned person. Yet here he was, willing to go—even excited at the thought of going—to a ball game where there would be thousands of strangers and who knew how many gawkers.

A friend of a friend of a friend with connections to the team had heard about the outing and arranged for Alvaro to get a private tour of the stadium while he was there.

"How about that?" the doctor asked.

"Can I bring Shawn?" Alvaro asked.

"Of course!" Benevento said.

The Mets played the Pittsburgh Pirates on that brilliant, sunny Saturday in Queens. The magic started the moment Alvaro and Shawn arrived at the ballpark. Alvaro, dressed in full Mets regalia over his bandaged torso, seemed bewildered when he and Shawn arrived at the ticket gate and were met by a man who introduced himself as a representative from the team. The man escorted them to the front of the line and through the gates into the stadium.

"This way," he said, pointing to the long tunnel leading to the ball field.

"We're going on the *field?*" Alvaro asked, his voice breathless with incredulity.

The man nodded.

"We're going to the field," Alvaro murmured.

Shawn, a Yankees fan, shrugged.

Alvaro hobbled through the tunnel. He was still frail. He stopped for a moment, with his mouth open, drinking in the scene before him. *I'm at Shea Stadium,* he thought. *There's the field. There's the dugout. Is this a dream?* A few feet away, the players were warming up. Bats swinging. Balls soaring. Cleats digging into the dirt. Dust flying. Alvaro took a few steps onto the grass. The only thing separating him from the players was the netting of the batting cage.

"The players would like you to be their guest on the field during batting practice," the man who worked for the team said.

"For real?" Alvaro said, barely able to catch his breath.

He looked at Shawn. Shawn's eyes were as wide as saucers.

"Okay," Shawn said. "I admit it. This is cool."

Alvaro grinned, then laughed a loud, hearty laugh.

A player approached. *Is he walking toward me?* Alvaro wondered. *No way. It can't be . . .*

"Hi. I'm Mike Piazza."

"I . . . I know," Alvaro said.

"Glad to meet you," the player said. "Can I shake your hand?"

Alvaro extended his gloved hand, and Piazza took it gently. "Hope you enjoy the game," the ballplayer said. "Get better."

"Okay," Alvaro said.

One by one, the players walked over and introduced themselves.

"Hi, I'm Derek Bell."

"I'm Edgardo Alfonzo."

"I'm Todd Zeile." Zeile lingered awhile, telling Alvaro and Shawn about his friend from high school who was burned doing a science project. "I know how much pain he suffered," the player said, and the boys nodded.

Bell and Alfonzo fetched two bats out of the dugout and scrawled their names with a black Sharpie on the blond wood. They handed one bat to Shawn, one to Alvaro.

"This is fantastic," Shawn said. "It doesn't get better than this."

Batting practice over, Bobby Valentine, the volatile team manager, appeared.

"How does your throwing arm feel?" he asked Alvaro.

Alvaro was unable to speak. *Is he talking to me?*

"Do you think you can throw the ball out?" Valentine asked.

"Do I *what?*"

Alvaro heard a familiar name over the public-address system. It was his name. Roger Luce, the Mets announcer, was introducing him and Shawn, describing them as "students from the Seton Hall fire."

The crowd roared.

Valentine positioned himself on the grass in foul territory, about ten feet from the top of the dugout steps, where the boys stood.

"Ready?" he asked.

First Shawn wound up and threw the ball to Valentine. "Nice throw," Valentine said, and the fans cheered.

Then it was Alvaro's turn.

Slowly he brought his arms up in front of him as far as his taut scars would allow, which was barely to his shoulders. Valentine stood by patiently. The stadium was quiet except for a jet passing overhead from nearby La Guardia

Airport. Alvaro stepped back with his left foot, turned toward the Mets manager, hesitated, then hurled the ball directly into Valentine's mitt. The crowd went wild.

Alvaro looked around the stadium. It looked as big as the earth, as tall as the sky. He wanted to freeze the moment, like a frame in a movie, never rolling forward, never winding back. If time stood still and he could stand here forever, he would.

The cheering of the fans brought Alvaro back.

"Nice toss," Valentine said, walking toward the dugout. Then, as if Alvaro were one of his players, Valentine smacked him on the backside.

Chapter 24

Angie Gutierrez ended her freshman year at Seton Hall with a 3.8 grade point average. Over the summer she made up an English course she had dropped after the fire, and she earned enough money working a part-time job to buy her first car. Things seemed to be going her way. In July, the university sent her to China for a week to attend an international conference of students. She made new friends and realized how much she loved to travel and how many interesting people there were to talk to. At home, in her spare time, she babysat for her younger siblings while her mother worked. All of that had left little time for Alvaro.

Angie's relationship with the Llanoses, which had once been so strong, had continued to deteriorate during the summer months. Daisy and Alvaro senior, who used to think of her as a third daughter, and who had once told people they couldn't ask for a better, more loving girl for their son, blamed her now for not spending more time with him, for not encouraging him to get better. She wasn't acting the way a girl in love was supposed to act, they said, nor did she seem like a girl who was planning on a future with their son. But Angie didn't think of herself as Alvaro's girlfriend, not anymore. She hadn't for quite some time. She was just a girl, she would say, at the beginning of an exciting new chapter in her life. She still cared deeply about Alvaro, and sometimes guilt clawed at her about moving on when he was trapped in a shattered world that might never be whole again. Some nights she didn't sleep at all, wondering, *Why can't I love him like I used to?* Alvaro's parents expected her to act like a wife, but she wasn't married and she didn't want that kind of attachment anyway, not to Alvaro, not to anyone. Although she planned to be a good friend to her former boyfriend, she didn't want to be tied down. She wouldn't allow herself to be. There was so much to see and do.

Alvaro's parents didn't understand. Sometimes weeks went by without a word from Angie. Not a telephone call. Not even a greeting card. Alvaro didn't say much about it, and each time someone brought it up he changed the subject, but Daisy knew his heart was broken. She could see it in his eyes when Angie's name was mentioned.

When Angie did finally show up at Kessler, after Alvaro had been there for three weeks, Daisy confronted her in the hallway and blocked her path before she could get to Alvaro's room. Daisy angrily demanded that Angie return Alvaro's gold crucifix ring, which Angie had worn on a chain around her neck since the fire.

"It's my son's ring," Daisy said. "You have no right to wear it."

At first, Angie said no, she wasn't giving the ring back, not unless Alvaro asked for it himself. Alvaro had told her to keep it, to wear it around her neck for as long as she liked, she argued, and until he said otherwise, that's what she planned to do.

Daisy seethed. "You don't love my son," she declared. "Now give back the ring and leave. Get out of here."

Angie pulled the chain from her neck.

"Here," she said, dropping the ring in Daisy's open hand. "Take it."

Both Angie and Daisy told Alvaro about the confrontation in the hallway. He felt caught in the middle. He loved and needed his parents. Who else would be there for him when he finally went home? Who else could he count on to be there, day and night, in the days and months ahead? To love him, burned? But he wanted to be with Angie, too. He understood her predicament, he told his mother. It was hard to take classes, study, and work and still find enough time to visit him.

"Stop," Daisy said. "You're making excuses for her."

Angie never returned to Kessler. Instead, she stayed in touch with Alvaro through daily telephone calls. The conversations were usually brief and chatty. *What'd you have for lunch today? How's your new car driving? What'cha watching on TV? Yeah. Okay. Talk to you later.*

When Angie complained bitterly that his parents had been unkind to her, Alvaro tried to defend them.

"They're just watching out for me," Alvaro said.

Angie said she still loved Alvaro. "But honestly, I'm taking this one day at a time."

What Angie didn't say was that she also felt anger toward Alvaro that she didn't quite understand. Sometimes at night, when she was alone in her bed, she felt abandoned by him. He hadn't been there for her all those months he was in a coma, when she was so afraid, more afraid than she had ever been before in her life, and needed him to comfort her, the way he had always comforted her after a scary movie. Even after he woke up, he had been distant. Sometimes, when she reached for him, he seemed to recoil. Other times, when she talked to him, he seemed not to listen, lost in whatever mindless show was on TV. Her father had been burned, and even as a little girl, she had felt the loneliness of his retreating into himself. All of a sudden he wasn't really there for his family anymore. He was there—he wouldn't even leave the house for fear of a stranger's stare—but emotionally he had disappeared. He had been burned, but everyone was trapped.

Sometimes, just before sleep, other thoughts crept into Angie's consciousness—thoughts she didn't want to think about, such as how Alvaro's burns really bothered her. Sometimes she had a hard time looking at him. He used to be so handsome. So strong. Now he was as feeble as an old man. Maybe she would get used to his altered state. But maybe she never would. And what would happen when they were out and people stared at him? Or worse yet, when people turned away completely, trying not to look? What would it feel like to be a spectacle? Or to be invisible? How could she think such things? she wondered. What kind of person *was* she?

"There are two kinds of affection," Angie told a friend one day. "I love Alvaro as a person, but I don't know if I'm in love with him anymore. So it's more of a friend thing with us right now. It's easier for both of us."

Angie turned melancholy as she spoke.

"If me and him don't end up together after all this, he'll find someone else and be okay," she said, turning her ring on her finger. "Because he's a great guy."

While Angie was trying to rationalize the end of the romance, Alvaro was still holding on to thoughts of a future together.

"I just hope everything works out," he said during a visit from Shawn one day. "I really hope that when I'm done with everything, we can get married. We both have to live our lives first, and we can't put pressure on each other. We have to have fun and see the world and learn more stuff because we're both so young.

"But even if we don't get married, I want to stay best friends, which I am. I am Angie's best friend."

Two months and five days after Alvaro entered Kessler, Dr. Benevento signed an order for him to go home. The first person he called was Shawn.

"Guess what?"

"You just signed with the Mets."

"Close. I'm going home."

"You're *what?*" Shawn's heart felt full.

In the past few weeks, Alvaro had begun walking better. His balance and endurance had improved. He could walk halfway around the gym without becoming so winded he had to stop. He could get up from a chair without help. His hands still trembled, but less so, so he could lift a fork to his mouth without the food falling off, and he could brush his own teeth, even though he still needed someone to squeeze the toothpaste from the tube onto the toothbrush. The fire had not ruined his smile. Alvaro's teeth were as white and straight as a brand-new picket fence, and he was proud of them.

Six months earlier, Alvaro had been near dead, and the doctors and nurses at Saint Barnabas had wondered if they were doing him a favor by keeping him alive. The fire seemed like forever ago to Alvaro, and at the same time like yesterday. Occasionally he wondered if he would ever know who had started it. He felt no animosity, no bitterness, toward the unknown arsonist—at least he didn't think so. He did want to be able to look the person in the face one day and ask why. But mostly, his thoughts centered on getting better and going home.

Now he was packing his sweats and his collection of Mets hats, all permanently stained from his long hours in the gym and the oozing of his burns, into a giant duffel bag. Alvaro knew that going home didn't mean the end of this painful chapter in his life story—hardly. Starting tomorrow he would have to return to Saint Barnabas for daily dressing changes and more physical therapy. But that meant reuniting with Roy Bond, and that made Alvaro smile.

He said good-bye to J. R., who had helped him build his strength and along the way became a cherished friend.

"This is just the beginning," J. R. said, hugging Alvaro. "There's still a lot of work to do. It's going to be up to you now."

"I'll miss you, man," Alvaro said. "But not too much."

They both laughed.

The day before, Benevento had left for her African safari, because for once everything had gone right. Alvaro had progressed better than anyone had expected. She signed his release form in advance and left him a note: "Hey kid, by the time you read this I'll be halfway to Africa, and you'll be on your way home. Stay in touch. You're awesome."

Alvaro folded Benevento's note and shoved it in his pocket. So many people had been so kind to him, had taken such good care of him, and he felt indebted to every one of them. He hoped that one day he would think of himself as just a person again, that his burns would be something he talked about in the past tense, and that when he did, people who hadn't known him as a burned person would say, *Oh! You were burned? Who would know?* Even if that didn't happen, he was determined to make the best of whatever lay ahead of him.

It was dinnertime when Alvaro and his parents began the half-hour trip from West Orange home to Paterson. They walked out of the rehabilitation center into a perfect, sunny afternoon and Alvaro's cherished blue Mazda. He hadn't seen his car for months, and his father had made sure it was buffed and shiny. Alvaro slipped into the front passenger seat, and his father slid into the back. His mother drove. First, they made a stop at Saint Joseph's Roman Catholic Church. Daisy had prayed there every day since the day of the fire. Now she thanked God for allowing her to keep her son when it had once seemed certain he would die. Alvaro senior prayed that his boy would one day be well enough to play baseball again. Alvaro prayed that going home would be everything he hoped it would be.

From the moment Alvaro could think clearly after awakening from his coma, all he thought about was going home. It was what had lifted him out of many funks and blue moods and motivated him when he was feeling too tired or too gloomy to work. Once he went home, he would tell himself over and over again, everything would be better. He could concentrate on his relationship with Angie, get back to his schoolwork, go out with his friends.

He was finally there.

Daisy blew the horn as she pulled up to the house on First Avenue. The first person Alvaro saw was Shawn.

"Hey, friend," Alvaro said. Shawn opened the car door.

"This is a very good day," Shawn said, helping to steady Alvaro as he got out of the car. Aunts, uncles, and cousins spilled out of the house and into the driveway, calling Alvaro's name and acting like an honor guard as he walked up the three wooden steps leading to the kitchen and another crowd of well-wishers. Pans of piping hot baked lasagna and chicken wings and rice and beans, Alvaro's favorite foods, waited on the table.

"Welcome home!" everyone shouted as he made his way through the doorway.

"It's good to be home," Alvaro said.

"It's good to have you home, Pápi," Alvaro senior said, wiping tears from his eyes.

That night, when the party was over and all of the guests were finally gone, Daisy showed Alvaro to his new room. It was the largest bedroom in the apartment, the one his older sister, Shirley, had once shared with her young daughter. While Alvaro was away, Shirley had moved into her own apartment so that Alvaro would have plenty of room during his recovery. Daisy had wanted it that way.

"Wow, this is great," Alvaro said, falling onto the bed. Within moments, he was fast asleep.

Alvaro slept in fits and starts that night. He woke up at midnight, frightened and unsure of where he was. When he fell back to sleep, he moaned and mumbled, his words incoherent and troubled.

Daisy was up all night, listening by his door. As much as she was happy her son was home, she was also terrified, and no amount of antidepressants or sleeping pills had been able to calm her. How would she care for Alvaro? she wondered.

He was still so weak, and his burns still bled. Just before he left Kessler, Alvaro had been getting out of his bed one day, and Daisy saw his bare back. She was shocked at how it looked after so many months, a mass of mutilated skin and open wounds. She had wanted to run out of the room and scream. How would her son live like that? How would he face the world with his distorted neck and his blighted face? How could she be reassuring now when she had a hard time just looking at his burns?

At least when Alvaro was in the hospital and at the rehabilitation center, she had been able to keep her worries from him, keep them for her own private moments at home when she would shut herself in her room and cry, or sit in the bathtub with the water running to drown out her screams. Even though her son was alive, she grieved for who he had once been, how he had once looked, and she was angry at the nameless, faceless person who had done this to him. Her bitterness and resentment were eating her alive. She couldn't let him see it. But how could she hide her feelings now, when he would be there all the time? Surely he would see the uncertainty in her eyes. Would he see the revulsion when she looked at his burns? *God help us,* she prayed.

Daisy watched the clock tick from midnight to daybreak. She could hardly wait to get Alvaro back to Saint Barnabas so that the professionals could take over again, even if it was for just a few hours.

Alvaro was supposed to be there early in the morning. Just getting him up and dressed was an ordeal, taking more than an hour. Nearly an hour after that, they were finally pulling into Saint Barnabas. The walk to the hospital from the parking lot seemed endless. Daisy and Alvaro senior had to keep stopping to wait for Alvaro to catch up. After greeting the nurses in the burn unit, Alvaro and Daisy headed for the tank room, where his wounds were scrubbed and his dressings changed. Mansour had agreed that Alvaro would be bathed every day at the hospital until Daisy felt comfortable cleansing and dressing his burns. Once the tanking was done, he headed downstairs for three hours of physical and occupational therapy.

The reunion with Bond was warm and happy.

"There's my man," Bond said, grabbing Alvaro in a bear hug. "You look great. You've come a long way."

Alvaro laughed. "What are you going to do to me today?"

"Just wait," Bond said.

Daisy and her husband hovered over Alvaro while Bond worked with him. When Alvaro had been a patient at Saint Barnabas, his therapy had been structured around visiting hours so that his parents weren't there. Now they sat and watched from the time they brought Alvaro in until it was time to take him home again. When Alvaro cried out in pain, Daisy winced and shrugged. Alvaro senior walked away, unable to abide his son's anguish. They interfered constantly, asking, *Do you need a drink of water? Is he hurting you? Do you want to stop now?*

The next day, they hovered even closer.

Are you okay, Alvaro? Does it hurt? Do you want to go home now? Roy, you're hurting him.

Bond asked Alvaro's parents to stay in the waiting room after that. They groused but did as they were told, reading magazines or walking the halls until it was time to go home.

Alone with Bond one day, Alvaro confided that his parents were suffocating him. He knew they loved him, but he couldn't go to the movies with friends without them coming along. The night before, Alvaro said, one of his cousins had offered to take him downtown to the movies. A few of the guys were going, and they thought it would be good for him to get out of the house. If anyone stared at him, they would stand in front of him, his cousin said, "so you feel comfortable." Alvaro decided to try it. When his cousin came to pick him up, Daisy grabbed her purse and followed them out the door.

"Where are you going, Mom?" he had asked.

"To the movies, with you," Daisy had answered, looking puzzled.

Bond listened and shook his head. "She's just trying to protect you, but it's too much," he said.

"I said, 'Mom, it's just the guys who are going.' And she started to cry," Alvaro explained. Daisy wanted to know what he'd do if something happened to him. His friends wouldn't know what to do. What if people looked at him? How would he feel without her there to protect him, defend him?

His parents did things for him that he should have been

doing himself, Alvaro complained. Sometimes he had to tell his father that he could feed himself.

"He picks up my fork and puts food on it and tries to feed me, like I'm a baby. When I'm eating, they keep watching to see if the food's going to fall off the fork, so then I get nervous and my hand shakes more and it does.

"They just won't let go," he concluded. "But I love them so much, I don't want to hurt them by saying anything."

"I know what you're saying," Bond said. "But you have to tell them sometime. They're feeling afraid. You're getting angry. And everyone's holding everything inside."

Finally, when Alvaro had been home for two weeks, the pent-up frustrations exploded.

Daisy was helping him take his first shower at home. She was nervous, afraid she might hurt him. Still weak and wobbly, Alvaro was leaning on a shower chair for support. Holding on with one hand, he soaped up with the other, while his mother attempted to cut the bandages off the top of his head. The gauze stuck. Daisy pulled. Alvaro cried out. She pulled harder. He cried out louder.

Finally, Alvaro pulled away from Daisy.

"I can do this myself!" he scolded her. "Let me do it on my own!"

Daisy was not accustomed to such anger from Alvaro. He had never been cross with her before. And he never talked back to his parents. He had certainly never raised his voice.

Trying to help Alvaro, she let go of the shower chair. It moved and he lost his balance. He nearly fell.

Alvaro pushed her away. "You don't know how to do anything!" he cried. "You don't do it like the nurses."

Daisy was stunned.

"Okay, then," she said, tears spilling from her eyes. "I'm not going to do anything for you anymore. I'm going to get a nurse to take care of you."

"What are you complaining about?" Alvaro wailed. "I'm the one who got burned!"

"I didn't want this to happen to you," Daisy cried, storming out of the tiny bathroom into her bedroom and slamming the door behind her. "It's not my fault that you got burned."

Daisy motioned the investigator toward a closed door off the living room of the tidy Paterson apartment.

"He's in there," she said shyly.

Frucci opened the door and squinted, trying to adjust his eyes to the darkened room. As he did, a shadowy figure came slowly into focus. The boy sitting on the bed wore an oversize sports jersey and baggy sweatpants. His hands were gloved, and a black knit mask covered his face except for his eyes and his lips, which were swollen and misshapen. A blue Mets baseball cap was pulled low over his forehead, not quite hiding the bloodstained gauze wrapped around his badly burned scalp.

"Are you Alvaro?" Frucci asked, standing in the doorway.

The boy looked up, then quickly averted his eyes. "Yes," he said quietly.

Frucci closed the door behind him.

"Hi. I'm John Frucci, the investigator from the prosecutor's office. It's great to see you, Alvaro. I've heard so much about you. Is it okay if we talk a little bit?"

"Sure," Alvaro replied, still looking away.

Frucci didn't show it, but he was shaken. The blinds on the windows were all drawn, blocking out the brilliantly sunny day. A TV droned with sports talk. A plate of rice and beans sat half-eaten on the dresser, next to a Coke can with a plastic straw protruding from it. The boy had sequestered himself in this darkened room, away from the possibility of prying eyes, and it looked as if he rarely left.

Frucci tried to be dispassionate about his work. He had been trained that way, after all. But looking at Alvaro, he wanted to cry. He had heard so much about the boy, about his kind heart and how he had always looked after his family. This all seemed so cruel, so unfair. With the flick of a lighter or a match, this happy, handsome young man had had his future annihilated.

"I have to ask you about the fire," Frucci said gently. "Everyone who was in the building that morning has been questioned, and I need to know what you remember about that morning."

"No problem," Alvaro said, glancing at Frucci. They talked for an hour or so. Matter-of-factly, Alvaro recounted the story of how he had fled from the dorm, but he had not seen or heard anything that could help the investigation.

Sitting with Alvaro made Frucci even more determined to prove who started the fire. He had had plenty of motivation before, motivation fueled by the smugness of students who had stonewalled the investigation. Suddenly, Ryan's fraternity brothers didn't remember saying certain things during those early interviews. They were either unavailable or obnoxious when investigators tried to speak to them. Some had been among the students subpoenaed during the raid on the bar a few months earlier, but there still was not enough evidence to present the case to a grand jury.

Sean Ryan and Joey LePore, meanwhile, had gone on with their lives as if nothing had happened. Ryan still attended Seton Hall. He partied at local bars and frat gatherings. LePore had transferred to the University of Delaware shortly after the fire, and investigators had kept an eye on him there. Sometimes they would take the three-hour ride down the New Jersey Turnpike and try to talk to his friends there. But they were just like Ryan's pals—arrogant and hostile. "Why are you doing this?" one girl asked a detective who approached her on the Delaware campus. "Why don't you just leave Joey alone?"

Frucci had been unnerved by the callousness of the students and by their complete disdain for authority. He wasn't all that much older than Ryan and LePore and their friends—a decade or so—and it would never have occurred to him, at that age, to thumb his nose at the cops or to lie about something so important.

Frucci couldn't help wondering, *Why did someone do*

this? And why won't they tell the truth? He wanted to think that there was some good in everyone and that one day these kids would say they were wrong and they were sorry. And he hadn't wanted to think people could be so bad that they didn't give a damn about what they did, even when their actions caused others to die.

Maybe they should see this boy, Frucci thought, looking at Alvaro. Maybe if they saw the damage they had done, saw the pain that had been inflicted, they would find a conscience.

Somehow, he doubted it.

He didn't think there was a conscience in the bunch.

At first, Alvaro had been against the idea of attending the burn support group meeting at Saint Barnabas. When Shawn first suggested it, Alvaro said he had all the support he needed from his family and his friends. Trying a different tactic, Shawn then said he didn't really need a support group, either. But maybe it wouldn't hurt to follow his mom's advice and try to help someone else.

"I mean, we know about what it's like to be burned," Shawn had said. "So why not share? Right? And think of it this way: we'll be the stars of the meeting."

Alvaro just laughed. He had no idea that his physical therapists had talked to Shawn, telling him that Alvaro seemed to be slipping in his recovery. He was getting too comfortable staying—hiding, they thought—in his house. Sometimes, Alvaro skipped therapy, his mother calling to say he wasn't feeling too well or he was just too tired. As many times as Bond had told Alvaro that it was his responsibility to phone when he wasn't coming, the messages still came from Daisy, and always very early in the morning when no one would be in the therapy room to pick up the phone. Sometimes Daisy called the night before, after everyone was gone for the day. "How do you know you're not going to feel good the night before?" Bond had asked Alvaro. "I don't know," he had replied, embarrassed by the question.

If they could just get Alvaro to come to the support group, Bond told Shawn one day during physical therapy, then they had a fighting chance of undoing the damage that was being done.

Shawn knew that the only way was to appeal to Alvaro's sense of selflessness and compassion for other people. Sure enough, after a few conversations with Shawn cajoling and badgering him, Alvaro finally gave in.

"Okay," Alvaro agreed. "But just one."

A dozen people were gathered in the burn unit's community room when Shawn and Alvaro arrived on that Tuesday at the end of August. Some were patients in the unit. Others were physically healed but struggling to survive in the real world: a firefighter who was burned while fighting a house fire years ago and seemed to be coping until his girlfriend lit a candle at dinner one night and he fell apart; a utility worker whose wife left him after he was burned by a rocket of flames that shot up out of a manhole; a woman who had dumped a pot of steaming soup on her chest as she lifted it into the freezer, and had terrible nightmares about being set on fire.

"This is Shawn Simons and Alvaro Llanos," said the social worker who led the meeting. Most of the others knew them from newspaper stories or television accounts of the dormitory fire, and just as Shawn had promised, they were treated like celebrities.

"I thought I read that you died," the mother of a burned child said to Alvaro.

"Almost," Alvaro said, fidgeting in his chair.

"Who has a question?" the social worker asked.

One mother, whose six-year-old boy was burned when he was playing with matches near a can of paint and it blew up in his face, worried about people staring at and ridiculing her child.

Shawn took the question.

"People do stare," he said. "Wherever I go. At the mall. In restaurants. In gas stations. Even in my own neighborhood, where everyone knows me. It's something I've had to learn how to deal with. Sometimes, when I see someone staring, I'll ask if they want to know what happened to me. They usually get all embarrassed, but I tell them anyway, and everything's cool. We both walk away feeling okay."

A man who was electrocuted while working on a train spoke: "I was in my car at a traffic light, and a man pulled up beside me and kept staring at me," he said. "I rolled down the window, looked over at him, and said, 'Boo!' "

Everyone laughed.

Another time, the man said, he was swimming at a public pool when he noticed someone staring. "So I turned to my buddy and I said, 'Jeez, I hope this leprosy is drying up.'"

Alvaro piped up.

People didn't just stare at him, he said. They gaped. "I can't hide my burns with a baseball cap and gloves the way Shawn does," he said. "I know people look at me and think I'm ugly. But then I have to think to myself that no matter what I look like now, I know I'm still me. I'm still the same person inside that I was before I got burned. And I'm going to get better in time."

The fire had taught him important lessons, Alvaro said, looking around the room. "I think I've learned more because of it. I've seen so much that other people haven't seen. I learned life is so precious, and no matter how bad things seem—say you don't have money, or you don't look the way you did once—well, you still have your life. That's what's important."

Pride washed over Shawn as he listened to Alvaro speak. This was Alvaro's moment, and as much as Shawn loved to be the center of attention, he was going to let him have it.

Shawn sat quietly when the next question came.

A little boy who was seated next to his mother waited for Alvaro to acknowledge him.

It was Jabrill, the eight-year-old who had been playing with matches when his bed caught fire, burning him over most of his body.

Admitted to the burn unit while Alvaro was there, Jabrill had turned to the teenager for comfort and encouragement. The relationship had continued, and he had recently telephoned Alvaro at home with a problem. The kids in the neighborhood were making fun of him because of the way he looked, Jabrill had explained. "Sometimes, when I go out with my mom, people stare."

"I think they're probably staring because you're so cute," Alvaro had said, and the little boy giggled. Alvaro had talked to him for an hour about ignoring children who were teasing him, finally soothing the young boy.

But the problem hadn't gotten better, Jabril said now. People still stared. He didn't know what to do.

People stared at him all the time, too, Alvaro explained. "Just the other day, I was standing in line at the movies, and this girl about my sister Shirley's age just stood there staring at me," Alvaro said. "I decided she was staring at me because *I'm* so cute."

Jabrill giggled again.

On the ride home from the hospital with Shawn, Alvaro was pensive.

"I need to get out more," he said.

"Yeah," Shawn said.

Alvaro watched the trees speed by, a rush of green with splashes of yellow and orange. Another season was about to end, and a new one would soon begin. For so long, all he had been able to think about was himself and getting better. It had to be that way. The task had been all-consuming, so there hadn't been time for anything else, or anyone else. Today, at the hospital, things had been different. He hadn't thought of himself or his troubles once, and it had felt good.

"I think I really helped people in there," Alvaro said, looking at Shawn. "I almost felt normal."

Shawn turned up the music on the radio.

"Told ya," he said.

Chapter 25

On the first day of the school year, shoving his burned hands into the pockets of his baggy Polo jeans and pulling a Yankees baseball cap over his forehead to hide the scars, Shawn returned to Seton Hall.

When Shawn left home that morning, Christine had felt like her son was going off to kindergarten for the first time. How would he feel once he was back on campus? Would he be able to adjust? Would he feel afraid? Shawn had assured her he'd be fine. The fire was in the past, and he didn't want to dwell on it anymore. What had happened, happened. It had made him a man. It had brought him closer to his father. And it had given him a new best friend. Shawn had stuck with Alvaro through the most difficult times of his life. He had celebrated with him when things went right, cried with him when everything seemed wrong. He was there the day Alvaro woke up from his coma. He had held his hand when he looked in the mirror for the first time.

When Alvaro moved from Saint Barnabas to the rehab facility, Shawn had been his first visitor. And his was the first face Alvaro saw when he finally came home.

Now, Alvaro wanted to return all those favors. He wanted to share this milestone with Shawn, to be there with him when he resumed college life.

Frail, scarred, and bandaged, Alvaro walked on campus, his parents tagging along behind him, searching for his roommate. The sun was brilliant, and students twittered with anticipation as they milled around, searching for their new classes. *I wish—*, Alvaro thought, dodging stares by turning his head or looking down at the ground, *I wish I was well enough, strong enough, to be back at school. I wish I had never been burned and it was me and Angie, holding hands, excited about beginning a new semester.*

"I wish I could find Shawn," he said to his parents, now scanning the faces of the students who passed him.

"I've counted four so far," Alvaro said as he walked. "Friends, people I knew pretty well—they didn't know who I was."

Alvaro called out to a girl. "Hey, it's me. How ya doing?"

"Al? Is that you? I wasn't sure," she said, running to him and hugging him gingerly.

"There he is!" Alvaro said, spying Shawn walking into a building a few feet away. "Shawn!"

"What are you doing here?"

"I wanted to be here for you, to wish you good luck on your first day back."

"Wow," Shawn said, his eyes filled with gratitude and pride that Alvaro had mustered the courage to come. "It's so great you came here, Al."

"I know," Alvaro said, and they both laughed.

Shawn headed for class, his first of five that day, and Alvaro headed for the parking lot, tired from the trip and ready to go home.

He couldn't help thinking that only a year ago, he had come to campus as an eager eighteen-year-old who had never spent a night away from his parents. His goals had been pretty straightforward: getting good grades, earning a spot on the school baseball team, and making a pretty girl named Angie Gutierrez happy.

Angie, who was living on campus again, seemed to be avoiding Alvaro lately. It had been days, probably longer, since she'd returned one of his phone calls. He had thought about her the night before, when he was planning his trip to Seton Hall to see Shawn. He mused about how much he loved her, and he wondered why he hadn't seen her and why she wasn't calling.

"I can't go home yet," Alvaro said to his parents as he took his cell phone from his pocket. "I'm going to call Angie to see if she's around."

Angie was agitated when she saw Alvaro in the lobby of her dormitory. She had not known he was on campus until he called to say he was there. "I'll be right down," she had said. She arrived in the lobby fifteen minutes later.

"Hi, sweetie," she said stiffly, ushering Alvaro and his parents to the courtyard outside. "I tried to call you yesterday," she said, kissing him on the cheek. "Really, I did."

The former lovebirds were ill at ease. They seemed to be dancing: Alvaro took one step forward, and Angie took one step back.

Mrs. Llanos looked away. Her heart was breaking.

A few minutes of chitchat later, Angie said she had to go. Alvaro and his parents headed for the car.

Taking refuge in the campus café, Angie slumped into an overstuffed couch. She wished it would swallow her up. Everything was so different now, Angie explained to a friend. "Sometimes it's not even him. It doesn't even look like him anymore. It's just hard to see him like that. I'm not embarrassed to be with him, but every time I see him I feel so bad. I'm afraid to talk to him about the relationship. Sometimes I feel like my life just stopped. I can't meet people. I guess I just want to move on. But I feel so guilty."

Other students had been scrutinizing Angie. "Even when I go out with friends, people say, 'How's Al?' They throw it in my face.

"In the beginning I was trying to be there for him. When he woke up from his coma, he wasn't communicating with me. Then he realized I was trying my best, but that wasn't good enough.

"I'm only nineteen," Angie continued, wringing her hands and staring into her lap. "I should be able to date other people.

I don't want people putting this on me, that I can't live because of Al. There's no right or wrong in this. I know a lot of people will disagree with that. They'll say I'm bad. I'm the type of person who, like, I hate it when people don't like me. But you can't judge someone unless you are in their position."

Angie had made a decision, she said. She would leave Seton Hall as soon as she could get accepted at a college in another state.

"I feel trapped here," she said. "The fire is going to haunt me forever. I have to deal with all of his friends watching me. If I was to go out with someone here, no one would accept it. I want to be there for him, but I just can't be there for him as a girlfriend. I want to be able to have the option to move on, and I don't feel like I have that option, and sometimes I resent that. I used to bug him all the time, 'When are we going to get engaged? C'mon, when, Al?' I really thought I would marry him. If this accident didn't happen, we would have gotten married and had kids and that would have been my life. But right now, he's not the one."

Angie started to cry.

"I sang to him when he was asleep for all those months, but he will never know about it. No one will know exactly what I went through. I guess my love left a while back when people were trying to keep me there. I've been trying to live on memories. I tried to stay so focused, to love him, to be there, but it's just not the same anymore. This is a love story that doesn't have a happy ending."

Two days later, Angie drove to Alvaro's house. He had asked her to come. He wanted to let her off the hook.

"I don't love you anymore," he said.

"Oh?"

"No. I'm sorry. I'd like to be your friend, but that's all I can be. I love you as a friend now. I hope that's okay."

Angie looked at Alvaro and saw her old boyfriend. She had never loved him more than at that moment.

"I understand," she said, hugging him tightly.

Alvaro turned and walked into the house. Angie got in her car and drove away.

Shawn was waiting in the Llanoses' house for Alvaro when he returned from talking to Angie. He had wanted to be there to catch him, if he needed someone.

"We talked the way we used to talk, and I know she still loves me," Alvaro said. "We decided to be real close friends for now. I have to become a man, and she has to become a woman. Then we'll see what happens.

"I'm not ready to be a boyfriend. I will do anything for her, but I can't hold her or take her away somewhere. It's not fair to her.

"Before she left, I told her that if she wasn't dating someone else when I got better, I would be there to take her back."

But Alvaro knew it would be a long time before he could put the fire behind him. His wounds were still healing and he faced years of surgeries to keep his scarring under control and his limbs from constricting. Pain was still part of his everyday existence and would be for the foreseeable future. As sorry as he had been to see Angie leave, he knew that letting her go had been the right thing to do. The passionate girl with the thick copper hair would be a hard act to follow. Angie had been his first and only love. She was smart and gregarious, and always challenging him. She wrote poetry, and she sang and danced. She was good for him. "And she's beautiful," Alvaro said, bowing his head. "To me, she's beautiful."

Chapter 26

Shawn awakened that brisk January morning feeling unsettled. It was the one-year anniversary of the fire. Sometimes it felt as if it had happened yesterday. Sometimes, it seemed like a lifetime ago.

Through his own fierce determination, Shawn had healed faster than anyone had expected. Although his hands would always be severely scarred, he had relearned to use them, and his facial scars were beginning to fade. A month earlier he had been discharged from therapy, three months ahead of schedule. He wanted to put the fire behind him.

But three boys were still dead, and his roommate struggled every day of his life. As much as Shawn would have liked to lock himself in his bedroom and sleep the day away, or go someplace far away and just try to forget everything, he owed it to them to be present at a memorial service commemorating the anniversary.

Shawn drove to the Seton Hall campus with conflicting

feelings of pride and dread. Pride in himself for hurdling so many obstacles over the past year. Pride in Alvaro for winning over death. Dread that he would have to face the parents of his dead classmates. How would his mother have felt had she lost him in the fire? He could only imagine the suffering of the families of Aaron Karol, John Giunta, and Frank Caltabilota. He didn't want to think about it.

Wearing a Yankees cap and a large gold cross around his neck, with his mother on his arm, Shawn strode into Walsh Gymnasium holding his head high. He had stopped wearing his gloves over his scarred hands most of the time. He knew people were watching. *There's Shawn,* they were certain to be saying, *one of the kids who was burned.*

The campus was dressed for the somber service. A large wreath with white roses and lilies was propped in front of a memorial bell tower that had been dedicated to the three dead students. A banner in the gym read, "We will never forget those who were lost. They will be with us forever. God is watching over this time of remembrance."

Alvaro, flanked by his parents, walked in a few minutes after Shawn and joined his former roommate and his mother in the front row of seats, which had been reserved for the victims and their families. He was still frail, but gaining strength. He looked around the gym. It was filled to overflowing. At least a thousand people had crowded onto the bleachers and into folding chairs, and everyone was wearing small metal lapel pins in the shape of a blue ribbon. John

Giunta had been a friend. He missed him. *Why did this have to happen?* he wondered. *Why did my classmates have to die?*

Shawn and Alvaro had heard the rumors swirling around campus—that fellow students had set the fire. They had read the newspaper stories saying investigators believed it was arson. And they wondered why no arrests had been made. Still, they felt almost no bitterness.

A week earlier, they had had a rare discussion about it, at Saint Barnabas, where Alvaro was recovering from surgery to loosen the leatherlike scars on his neck, which had limited his head movement.

Somehow the conversation had turned to the fire. "I don't know who set it, so there's nobody to be angry at," Shawn said. "I don't know how I'll react if there is a name. You can't go around hating someone you don't know. But whoever did this, I don't think they were trying to hurt anybody. It's like getting hit with a stray bullet. They weren't aiming for me."

Alvaro nodded. He used to think a lot about the fire, he acknowledged, and to wonder how it happened, but he didn't much anymore.

"I used to get mad because these kids did something so stupid," he said. "I think they probably lit a fire and it got out of control. Something little got real big. I still get mad when I think about the three boys who died. It makes me feel sad to think of how much their families are hurting. But the kids who died are in heaven now, so at least they're safe."

"That's true," Shawn had said.

Shawn thought back on that conversation with Alvaro as he waited for the memorial service to begin. *What's the sense of being angry?* he thought. *It won't bring the dead boys back. Or erase our scars.* He remembered something Alvaro had said: "Sometimes I think I am one of God's angels, sent down to do good. Maybe to help people who are not as strong as I am."

Monsignor Robert Sheeran walked to the microphone, and the gymnasium fell silent.

"This has been a year of brutal loss and terrible consequences," he began. "Our families have lost more than we should ever have to. But you have not lost everything. You have not lost the blessings of each other nor the friends that stand by your side."

Shawn looked at Alvaro. Alvaro looked back. They had talked often about moving back on campus one day and had decided they probably would, but only when Alvaro was better and they could live together again. From that first day at Seton Hall, when Alvaro had picked Shawn out of all the other freshmen milling around campus and told his parents, "I think he's going to be my roommate," he had known theirs would not be an ordinary relationship. "There's something different about me and Shawn," he had later told a friend. "I don't know what it is. We don't even have to talk. I sense his strength, and it makes me strong, too."

Sometimes I think I am one of God's angels, sent down to do good. Maybe to help people who are not as strong as I am.

Monsignor Sheeran continued to speak. "One year ago, our hearts were broken wide open," he said. "But now listen to the sound of our hearts healing."

Shawn bowed his head. "Let it be," he whispered in quiet prayer. "Let it be."

Chapter 27

After eighteen months of stonewalling by the two prime suspects, investigators went to court to get a warrant to bug Joey LePore's house.

The Essex County prosecutor's office had recently gotten a tip that LePore's mother, Maria, had allegedly spoken to a friend about her son's involvement in the fire. The tipster wasn't a typical citizen. He was Thomas Ricciardi, a Mafia hit man and now a professional snitch. Eight years earlier, Ricciardi, who had admitted to playing a role in nine murders, had been convicted of beating an associate from the Lucchese crime family to death with a golf club. Facing forty years in prison, he flipped, offering to tell the federal authorities everything he knew about the mob in exchange for a plea agreement that would lock him up for only ten years instead of life. Since then, Ricciardi had been a valuable tool for the government. With his help, the feds had been able to put away members of the Lucchese, Colombo, and Genovese crime families.

In the middle of his ten-year sentence, Ricciardi sent word to the Essex County prosecutor that he had information about the Seton Hall fire. Investigators met with him at the federal prison where he was being held, and a deal was struck. The prosecutor's office would do whatever they could to cut time off the five remaining years of Ricciardi's federal prison term in exchange for his information.

Ricciardi told prosecutors that his brother, Daniel "Bobo" Ricciardi, was dating a woman who was friendly with Joey LePore's mother, and that he believed Maria LePore may have discussed her son's role in the fire. The story was enough to persuade the judge to issue the warrant to place a hidden listening device in the house on Woodbine Road in Florham Park, a leafy bedroom community in one of New Jersey's wealthiest counties.

Investigators quietly broke into the LePores' home on the eve of the Fourth of July, 2001. They had nothing to lose. They had conducted 220 interviews and taken 150 sworn statements, and they were still no closer to an arrest than they had been on the day of the fire. Joey LePore had steadfastly denied he was even in the third-floor student lounge the night the fire broke out. Sean Ryan had never spoken to investigators after that first day in the South Orange police headquarters. And their friends weren't talking, either.

While the LePores enjoyed a summer afternoon in New York City, detectives placed the bug in their kitchen and a tap on their phone before slipping back out without leaving a trace.

All that was left to do was sit back and listen.

Despite what they had been through together, Shawn and Tiha found themselves drifting apart. Two years after the fire, they decided to go their separate ways. Four months later, Tiha contacted Shawn to say she was pregnant. *Why is this happening now?* he wondered. *Now, when we're both so young and trying to concentrate on school? We said we would stay friends, but do we want to be a couple again?*

As it turned out, Tiha was having the same anxieties. She and Shawn had started out as friends, and she had hoped they would always be friends. But it had only been a few months since they decided to break up. She had been enjoying college life and meeting new people and all of the other adventures that had come with this new chapter in her life. She wasn't at all sure she wanted to go back.

"What are we going to do?" she asked Shawn.

On a perfect spring night in May, Shawn and Tiha sat down together to discuss their options. The talk was cordial and warm. They decided to stay close but to raise their child apart, and they parted that night with a hug and a vow to always be kind to each other, for the sake of their child.

That fall, Shawn was driving to a friend's birthday party in Manhattan when Tiha called to say she was having contractions.

"I'm on my way to the hospital," she said. "Can you meet me at Saint Barnabas?"

"I'm on my way," Shawn replied, making a sharp U-turn at the mouth of the Lincoln Tunnel and racing back toward the hospital.

Tiha's labor was hard and long. Shawn held her hand and wiped her forehead with a cool cloth, trying to soothe her. Both of their mothers were there. Almost twenty-four hours after Tiha called Shawn, she was finally ready to give birth.

"Push!" the doctor said. "C'mon now, Tiha, you're almost there. Push!"

Tamir DeShawn Simons was born a few seconds past five o'clock on October 27, 2002. The first thing Shawn saw was the black ringlets that covered his son's tiny head. They looked just like his curls before the fire. *This is the best moment of my life,* Shawn thought as he looked at his son. It hadn't been that long ago that Shawn had lain in a coma, two floors down, the promise of a future uncertain.

Shawn looked at Tiha through his tears.

"I promise that no matter what happens between us, I will always be there for my son," he said.

Tiha smiled. "I believe you," she replied.

It was a promise Shawn knew he would keep.

Panic pricked at Alvaro's skin when he realized what had happened.

He had ventured out a few times lately, always at his friends' insistence, but tonight he hadn't wanted to go. Why, he wondered, had he let them talk him into coming to a *dance club,* anyway? He was too afraid to approach girls. He was certain that he would be rejected, or that he would make them feel so uncomfortable, they would feel they had to talk to him. He didn't want that.

His friends wouldn't take no for an answer, though. He needed to get out and start living his life again, they said. They would be there for him. They would walk him to the bathroom, walk him to the bar. Wherever he went, they would shield him from the stares of strangers.

But now he was in the middle of a pack of writhing dancers, under flashing colored lights, alone and terrified. Somehow he and his friends had become separated.

The summer air was thick with humidity, and the club was thicker with cigarette smoke. Alvaro felt as if he might suffocate. A red exit sign shone in the distance, and with his head down, he made his way toward the open door. A big, bulky bouncer stood in front of it, expressionless, staring straight ahead. "You can't go out this way," he said sternly, never even looking at Alvaro.

Alvaro stood to the side of the bouncer, closer to the door and the outside air. If he started to hyperventilate or it all just became too much, he could duck out the door before the security guard caught him, then wait in the dark of the parking lot for his friends to come out.

A Marc Anthony song blared from the loudspeakers. Alvaro, clad in his usual blue Mets baseball cap and an oversize sports jersey, tried to concentrate on the lyrics, but it was no use. He was certain everyone in the room was staring at him, and he fought the urge to run and hide. Maybe it was dark enough in the club that no one could see him—see his scars, anyway. He dared to take a quick look around for his friends. Sure enough, a girl was staring at him. He looked away. *If she's still looking, I'm out the door,* he thought. He glanced back at the girl. She was pretty, very pretty, with melancholy eyes and long auburn hair, like Angie.

She beckoned him with her finger. *Did she really?*

He turned to look behind him, but no one was there. Only the wall.

She beckoned him again.

He pointed his finger at his chest. *Me?*

The girl nodded, and before he had the chance to run out the door, he saw that she was gently pushing her way past the people on the dance floor, headed straight for him.

Alvaro felt streams of perspiration drip from his forehead and down the side of his face and neck. His baseball cap was damp and he couldn't catch his breath. Two and a half years had passed since the fire, and he was far from healed. His torso was still so raw it had to be wrapped in gauze to keep his wounds from becoming infected and to prevent blood from oozing through his clothing. His face, arms, and hands were a red and brown patchwork of thick scars and skin grafts. Alvaro thought he was ugly.

The petite girl stood there, looking up at him. "Hi, I'm Paula," she said. "You're Alvaro, right?"

"Yeah," he said, clearing his throat nervously and looking from the girl's eyes down to his feet.

"I went to high school with your sister Shany. You were two years ahead. You probably don't remember me."

"No," Alvaro quietly admitted.

She remembered him, though. All of her friends at John F. Kennedy High School in Paterson twittered about Shany's older brother. *Alvaro is so hot,* the girls would say, and Paula would agree because he was.

"I heard you were burned," she said. "My mom read stories about it in the paper."

"Yeah," Alvaro replied.

"Do you mind if I stay and talk to you?" she asked.

"No. That would be fine."

"Do you want something to drink?"

"A water would be good."

"Okay. I'll get us two waters," she said, heading for the bar. When she returned, the two sipped bottled water and tried to think of things to say.

"Would you like to dance?" she asked finally.

"Uh . . ."

"Oh, c'mon. It'll be okay."

"Okay."

The music played on and they started to dance, right there by the open door, away from the crowd dancing under the flashing lights. It was the first time Alvaro had held a girl in his arms since before the fire. He had feared he never would again. Paula felt good in his arms. She fit perfectly. One song turned to several songs. An hour passed. Then two.

Alvaro's eyes were closed. All of a sudden, he felt like he was riding on a carousel. It was the two of them and the room was spinning around them, just like in a dream sequence from a movie. For a moment he forgot where he was. For a moment he forgot he was burned.

Then the music stopped and the room lit up. Last call, announced someone.

"I gotta go," Alvaro said, avoiding the girl's gaze under the bright lights that signaled closing time. "Can I call you sometime?"

The two exchanged numbers.

"I'd really like to talk again," Paula said.

Yeah, sure, Alvaro thought, then quickly answered: "Me, too."

He did.

Chapter 28

Alvaro was falling in love.

He knew it, knew it as surely as he could know anything. But what about Paula? The question was keeping him awake at night. He couldn't sleep for worrying about whether she could really love someone who had been through what he had.

It had been Paula who called *him* after they first met in the dance club. She told him she went home that night and dropped into bed without even changing into her pajamas. She kept her cell phone beside her in bed, wishing he would call. When she awakened the next morning, her stomach quivered with excitement, thinking they had spent hours on the telephone talking about everything and nothing. But she quickly realized she had dreamed the conversation. She had even checked her cell phone to make sure he hadn't called, but there were no messages and no missed calls. After stewing awhile, she made up her mind to call. She didn't care how pushy or desperate she looked. She really liked him.

"I had to talk to you again," Paula had said when he answered her call.

Since then, they had spent almost every day together. When they weren't taking a drive or watching TV in his room, they were talking on the phone. One week had passed, then another.

Alvaro knew Paula *liked* him. She had told him many times that he was the sweetest boy she had ever met. But could she love someone like him? If she couldn't, wouldn't it be better to know now? But did he really want to know? Did he want to know the reason if she couldn't love him?

Finally he decided he had to act. Pulling up his shirt so that she could see just a glimpse of his gnarly, knotted stomach, Alvaro took a deep breath and asked, "Do you think you can handle this?"

Paula had given the question plenty of thought. Alvaro hadn't been the first to ask.

Her own mother had pulled her aside one day. "What are your intentions with this boy?" she had asked. "Don't play with his heart, Paula. He's a nice boy and he's been through enough."

After that, her older brother put in his two cents, saying, "You don't want to hurt this kid, do you? You don't know what you're getting yourself into. You can't handle this."

"I think I can," she told him.

"I know I can," Paula told Alvaro, now that he was the one who was asking. "I look past the burns and see the person," she told him.

They had made love after that. Alvaro told Paula, "I want to keep my shirt on." So Paula kept hers on as well. The first time was awkward, painfully so. Alvaro was disappointed. Paula comforted him. *Don't worry. It will get better. It'll be okay.*

Days passed. They made love again. It was better. After that, they took it slowly.

Paula asked permission to explore his body underneath his clothes. He unbuttoned part of his shirt and she touched his chest and his arms.

"I love your arms," she said. "They're so soft."

Each time, he trusted her a little more.

"I want to see how your skin feels against mine," Paula said one night when they were together in Alvaro's bed.

Alvaro felt his heart beat wildly. "I don't know," he said.

"Don't be embarrassed," she said soothingly. "It'll be all right."

Slowly he unbuttoned his shirt and pulled it away from his scarred chest. He unzipped the special vest that exerted pressure on his burned skin. He was naked, and trembling.

Tears filled Paula's eyes. She pulled him close to her.

"You're beautiful," she whispered.

The telephone call came from a detective in the Essex County prosecutor's office on the evening of Tuesday, June 10, 2003. The sound of a gruff voice surprised Shawn. He had been expecting to hear from his new girlfriend, a pretty girl named Chinaire, whom he had known casually in high school and recently met up with again at a club in Newark. Sparks flew after he asked her to dance, and they had been spending a lot of time together. They had a date planned and she was supposed to call to tell him what movie she wanted to see.

Instead he was listening to a detective telling him that arrests in the Seton Hall fire were imminent. It had been 1,238 days since the fire. This was a courtesy call, the detective said. "We didn't want you to be caught off guard."

"What about Alvaro?" Shawn asked. "Does he know?"

"We're trying to reach Alvaro, too," the detective said.

Shawn didn't sleep much that night. Every time he looked at the clock, it was only a few minutes later. After more than three years, he thought he had put the fire behind him. At least that's what he told himself and everyone else. But after the phone call from the detective, awful memories he'd locked deep within began to wash over him like a tidal wave, and he hadn't been able to catch his breath. He had tried calling Alvaro but hadn't gotten an answer. He hoped his old roommate knew the news.

Lying there, all alone in his bed, Shawn wondered if it would have been better if no one had been caught. That way, he would have gone on pretending it didn't matter much who set the fire. Somehow, without a name and a face to focus on, it had been easier not to blame anyone, to think it was just a terrible accident and no one was really responsible. Tomorrow he would have both a name and a face, and he wasn't sure how he would feel.

The arrests of Joey LePore and Sean Ryan the following

day made headlines around the country. Ryan was picked up as he was leaving a tanning salon near his home. LePore was pulled over in his car near his home in Florham Park.

The cops showed more emotion than the suspects as they led the pair, handcuffed and shackled, with their heads bowed, into the county jail at about six that night. John Frucci had tears of relief in his eyes as he escorted them from the unmarked police car to the jail. It had been a long, hard investigation. The suspects had stonewalled law enforcement officials every step of the way, and Frucci had often thought there might never be an arrest in the case.

The *Newark Star-Ledger* reported that a special grand jury had been meeting behind closed doors in the Essex County Courthouse in Newark every Thursday for a year and a half. They had heard testimony from hundreds of witnesses, including students, firefighters, and arson investigators, and pored over more than six thousand pages of statements and exhibits. By the time the proceedings were finally over, one of the grand jurors had died and several others had been excused because of illness or work problems.

What the grand jury heard over those long months was that Ryan and LePore had had a reputation in Boland Hall. One of the students had dubbed them Beavis and Butt-Head. On the night of the fire, after the biggest basketball game on Seton Hall's schedule, a freshman girl and her roommate threw a party in their room on the third floor in Boland Hall, on the other side of the building from Shawn and Alvaro's room. Ryan and LePore attended the party. It was raucous and spilled over into the third-floor lounge. A few of the boys were roughhousing, and a playful wrestling match broke out between Ryan and one of his fraternity brothers. A resident adviser named Dan Nugent, who had had previous run-ins with Ryan and LePore, threw everyone out of the lounge at around four in the morning, thirty minutes before the fire.

LePore and Ryan's next-door neighbor in Boland Hall was John Giunta. Giunta's roommate testified that after the commotion in the lounge quieted down, he heard two sets of footsteps running into and then out of Ryan and LePore's room. The next thing he heard was the fire alarm wailing.

The case against LePore and Ryan was far from ironclad. But what had turned it from hopeless to possible for prosecutors was testimony from a reluctant witness named Michael Karpenski. Karpenski, a childhood friend, had partied with Ryan and LePore in Boland Hall in the hours before the fire. In early interviews with investigators, he had admitted being in the dorm that night but said he knew nothing about how the fire started, or who set it.

After testifying before the grand jury, however, Karpenski contacted investigators to say he had forgotten to tell them something. That "something" turned out to be the closest thing prosecutors had to clear evidence of guilt.

At a meeting at the prosecutor's office, Karpenski recalled that two days after the fire, he was summoned to the Dunkin' Donuts in Madison by Ryan, LePore, and Tino Cataldo, another friend who was with them in Boland Hall on the night of the fire. The boy told police investigators that the four friends had made a pact in the Dunkin' Donuts on that Friday afternoon in January of 2000. Karpenski said they vowed they would not tell police anything about what was going on in the third-floor lounge before the fire.

Surveillance tape from an all-night fast-food restaurant confirmed that Karpenski and Cataldo had left the dorm at least an hour before the fire started. Even though Karpenski wasn't in the lounge when the match was struck, investigators believed he knew what happened there after he left.

Karpenski was brought back to the grand jury, where he testified about the secret meeting. Prosecutors still couldn't prove Ryan and LePore lit the banner, but they felt the clandestine meeting raised the question: if Ryan and LePore had nothing to hide, why call a meeting about the fire?

The grand jury obviously agreed.

Ryan and LePore were charged with arson, aggravated assault, reckless manslaughter, and felony murder. The felony murder charge carried a minimum sentence of thirty years in prison. Bail was set at $2 million each. At the bail hearing, LePore turned to the news cameras and smirked.

Separate indictments accused LePore's parents and sister of covering up his role in the fire. The indictments revealed that the listening devices detectives had concealed in the LePores' kitchen had picked up at least nine conversations about the fire. During one of those talks, LePore's father discussed the possibility of taking the family out of the country rather than risking the chance that Joey might be charged. The next day, Maria LePore had urged her husband and children to lie to investigators and "stay united." No one was going to hurt her boy.

The detective who called Shawn had not been able to reach Alvaro to warn him of the arrests. Instead, the next day, as he was driving to a store to buy a stereo, he got the news from a friend who called him on his cell phone.

"I'm going to have to stop now to take this all in," he said, pulling his new black Acura with black tinted windows to the side of the busy highway.

A photograph in the next day's newspaper showed Ryan and LePore being led to jail. Shawn sat alone at his kitchen table and studied the picture. He recognized the boys as the students who had lived right across the hall.

Chapter 29

Shawn graduated from Seton Hall on May 10, 2004, with a degree in business management. He was among more than two thousand graduates at the commencement ceremony at Continental Airlines Arena in East Rutherford. Sitting in the arena, under a huge net of blue and white balloons, with his parents, his sister, Nicole, and his girlfriend, Chinaire, looking on, he thought about how far he had come since the fire. He thought about the dedication of his mother, whose optimism and determination had left him no choice but to reclaim his life. He thought about his three classmates who had died in the fire, who never got a chance to fulfill their dreams. He thought about Alvaro. *I wish he was here, sitting right next to me in his cap and gown.*

Alvaro would have been there if he could. But he was lying in a hospital bed at Saint Barnabas, recovering from another skin graft surgery, this time on his neck. It was his twenty-third birthday, but he wasn't thinking about birthday cake or gifts. He was thinking about Shawn. What better way to celebrate than to think about his former roommate finally reaching his dream?

"I'm so happy for Shawn," Alvaro told a friend who was visiting. "I wish I was there with him. But he's finishing and I'm starting. I'll get there, too."

Alvaro had his own good news to share. A day earlier, in his hospital room at Saint Barnabas, he had gotten down on one knee and proposed marriage to Paula. Her answer was, "Of course!" Hani Mansour had been the first person on the staff to congratulate them. "A wedding!" he had exclaimed. "Look how far you've come, Alvaro! When will we see children?" Alvaro and Paula had often talked of having a big family someday, but Paula found herself pregnant sooner than they had planned. Many of her friends had children born out of wedlock, but Paula was determined to be married when she gave birth. "Marriage is important to me," she had told Alvaro. "I want to be married when our child is born." Alvaro was happy to oblige her.

A month after the engagement, on June 26, 2004, Paula and Alvaro married in a small ceremony at Paterson City Hall. Paula wore a pretty white pants suit with pink flowers that Daisy had bought for her. Alvaro dressed in a black shirt and khaki-colored trousers. Only their families attended. The ceremony was simple but emotional.

"Do you take this man to be your lawfully wedded husband?" the judge asked Paula.

"I *do,*" she answered, fighting back tears.

"Do you take this woman to be your lawfully wedded wife?" he asked Alvaro.

Alvaro grinned from ear to ear. He had never been so absolutely sure of anything before in his life.

"I do," he said softly, looking into Paula's eyes. "I *do.*"

Five months later, at 11:47 P.M. on November 28, 2004, Ariana Izabella Llanos was born at Saint Barnabas. Everyone in the burn unit cheered when word filtered upstairs. Paula had gone into labor while making bows for the family Christmas tree. She sang all the way to the hospital. The birth was fast and relatively easy. Alvaro videotaped the whole thing. The waiting room outside the maternity unit was overrun with Llanos and Vasqucz family members.

Waiting for her granddaughter to be born, Daisy couldn't help remembering those somber days in the burn unit. Those nights wondering if she would ever get to touch her son again, ever get to hear him say he loved her. Even after Alvaro was out of danger, she and her husband had been consumed by worry that Alvaro would never find love, never have children, never enjoy the simplicity of a normal life again.

Then he had found Paula, and everything had changed.

"¡Gloria a Dios, hay razón para ser feliz otra vez!" Daisy prayed that night.

Glory to God. There is reason to be happy again.

Alvaro shut himself in his bedroom and began writing.

> *These seven years have been hard for my family and me; this tragedy has given me many obstacles to overcome. I will always remember the day of the fire, waking up to alarms and smoke, trying to find a way out of the building, fearing for my life. I'm reminded every morning of this when I look at my face in the mirror. My body is covered with scars . . .*

A few weeks earlier, just before opening arguments in their arson and felony murder trial were about to begin, Joseph LePore and Sean Ryan had struck a plea deal with prosecutors. After three years of being free on bail, they had exhausted all their appeals. Rather than leave their fate in the hands of a jury and risk spending the better part of their lives behind bars, they would admit to setting the dormitory fire in exchange for five-year jail terms and a chance at parole after sixteen months. For their part, the prosecutors had feared the case against LePore and Ryan might not hold up at trial and they would walk away free. The plea deal brought about an abrupt end to a case that had seemed destined for a long, dramatic trial.

Sipping tea in the kitchen of the burn ICU, Hani Mansour had read the headline and thought back to the worst day in the burn unit's history. He looked up from his newspaper and into room 4. It didn't seem that long ago that Alvaro had lain there, fighting for his life. Now the bed was empty.

The next day, Friday, January 26, 2007, LePore and Ryan would be sentenced, and Alvaro would get his chance to ask why.

Why did you set the lounge on fire? Why did you run out of the building without warning all of us? Why did you lie and deceive everyone for all those years, living your lives, going to college, kissing your girlfriends, celebrating Christmas and birthdays with your families, instead of admitting that you had done something stupid, so tragically stupid? Instead of saying you were sorry. So very sorry.

Shawn had decided not to attend the sentencing. He wasn't sure he wanted to be in the same room with LePore and Ryan. He was feeling some anger and didn't know how he would handle it.

"I'm not going," he told Alvaro on the phone that night. "I'm sorry. I can't."

So it would be up to Alvaro to speak. This would be the last big step of the most painful journey of their lives, and he would take it for both of them. He would do it for himself, and he would do it for Shawn—Shawn, who had been there for him at every turn. When he woke up from his long coma. When he looked in the mirror for the first time. When things ended with Angie. His former roommate had become a cherished friend.

As Alvaro tried to put his thoughts on paper, his heavily scarred hands still shook from the exertion. But he would not be deterred. He wanted those two boys to know the damage they had done, how much heartache they had caused for him and for Shawn and for the dead boys, too—for all the people whose lives were forever changed by Ryan and LePore's one stupid act.

It saddens me to hear what my family had to go through, seeing me in a coma for so long, not knowing if I would be alive when they got there the next morning. When I finally did wake up, I couldn't speak or walk. I was connected to machines. It was scary for me. I had so many ups and downs. To this day I have times when I don't want to step out the door, when I feel trapped in my own skin.

Two hours later, Alvaro emerged from his room with a single sheet of paper that reflected seven years of suffering.

To this day I have times when I don't want to step out the door, when I feel trapped in my own skin.

After a sleepless night, Alvaro and his family drove to the courthouse in Newark in silence. Alvaro trembled during the whole forty-minute ride. Paula draped her arm protectively over his shoulder as they huddled together in the backseat. Alvaro's heart raced wildly and he felt as though he might be sick.

The ninth floor of the Essex County Courthouse swarmed with news crews volleying for the best seats in the small courtroom where the formal plea proceeding would take place. The left side of the room was reserved for victims; the right side, for supporters of the defendants. It was standing room only in the sweltering courtroom, and the tension was thick as people jostled for a spot. Alvaro sat toward the front of the courtroom, near the parents of the boys who died. They all hugged him. A moment before the proceedings were about to begin, LePore and Ryan walked through the overflow crowd in the hall and into the courtroom. LePore stopped to kiss his girlfriend on the way. Both men turned to greet family members and friends with hearty hellos and wide smiles. Alvaro looked at them and suddenly felt sicker. *How can they be smiling? What is wrong with them? Don't they know the parents of the dead boys are here?*

Judge Harold Fullilove called the court to order. The room fell still. Frank Caltabilota Sr., whose son died in the fire, was the first of fourteen victims to speak. "Mr. LePore and Mr. Ryan, I have waited exactly seven years and one week to tell you both what I think of you and how your stupid prank that got out of hand has affected myself and my family."

Under the plea agreement, the prosecutors had agreed to drop the most serious charge—that of felony murder. LePore and Ryan agreed to plead guilty to arson and witness tampering. By accepting the plea, they were spared the minimum thirty-year prison term they would have gotten had they gone to trial and been convicted of murder. The prosecutors also dropped the obstruction of justice charges against LePore's family. The five-year sentence was a joke, Frank Caltabilota said, echoing the feelings of most of the victims. Their true punishment would come later, he said. "That sentence, Mr. LePore and Mr. Ryan, will be that both of you rot in hell." The defendants' families and friends were expressionless, completely dry eyed.

Alvaro turned to look at LePore and Ryan. He could see their profiles and wanted them to turn to their left to meet his eyes, to look at his scarred face, to see the anger in his eyes. He wondered if he would see something in their eyes. Sorrow? Regret? But they didn't look, and now it was his turn to speak and the room began to spin. Seven years of pent-up emotion circled in his head, and his eyes began to tear.

"I can't do it," he whispered to Paula. "I can't."

Squeezing Alvaro's hand, Paula took the piece of paper from his lap and walked to the front of the courtroom. She swallowed hard and then began reading from the paper, which shook in her hand. Now Paula was speaking for him. "*My heart goes out to all the families who have lost family members in this tragic fire,*" she said, reciting Alvaro's words before bursting into tears. Then Alvaro burst into tears, too.

Paula was helped back to her seat by a sheriff's officer. She buried her head in Alvaro's shoulder and sobbed while the prosecutor picked up the paper and began where she had left off.

"*Right now I can't see myself ever forgiving these two kids for starting this fire,*" the prosecutor said, reading the words Alvaro had written in the privacy of his room the night before. "*If it was a mistake, they should have been man enough to bang on people's doors and save everyone's life. Instead, they ran off like the cowards that they are. One question I have always wanted to ask is why. What was your reason for starting this fire?*"

It was a question that would not be answered. Not now, not in this courtroom. Maybe not ever. When it was their turn to speak, LePore and Ryan recited similar statements.

"I, along with Sean Ryan, lit a banner on fire that was draped across the couch in the third-floor lounge of Boland Hall. There's nothing I can do to take your pain away," LePore said, looking straight ahead at the judge. "I'm sorry."

"I am very, very sorry," Ryan said, glancing toward Alvaro and the families of the dead, then quickly looking away. "I hope you can move on."

Ninety minutes after the proceeding had begun, it was over. LePore and Ryan were led out of the courtroom in handcuffs and shackles. Their loved ones wailed. They did not look back.

If they had, they would have seen Alvaro wiping away his tears.

Shawn picked up the phone on the first ring. It was Alvaro. He knew it would be.

"I couldn't do it," Alvaro said. "I tried, but I broke down."

"I know," Shawn said. "I was watching on TV. I'm proud of you, Al. You went. You were the strong one."

"It's over," Alvaro said.

"Yes," said Shawn. "It's over."

Epilogue

Alvaro and Paula Llanos have two children, a girl and a boy.

Shawn Simons has two sons. He is engaged to Chinaire Fields.

Both Shawn and Alvaro work at the *Star-Ledger* in Newark, New Jersey.

Hani Mansour is still the director of the Saint Barnabas Burn Center. He continues to dream of one day returning to Beirut to open a burn unit there.

John Frucci is no longer investigating fires. When the Seton Hall fire investigation concluded, he asked to be transferred out of the arson unit. He now works homeland security.

Sean Ryan was paroled in May 2009 after serving twenty-eight months of his five-year sentence. "The state parole board denied parole to Sean Ryan at his first eligibility on March 31, 2008. Today, after a thorough hearing lasting approximately an hour and fifteen minutes, the state parole board determined that Sean Ryan meets the legislative standard for release to parole supervision," said Neal Buccino, a parole board spokesman, in a prepared statement. Ryan had been "a model prisoner."

Joseph LePore, who was also denied parole at his first eligibility hearing, will appear before the board again in November 2009.

Acknowledgments

Let me begin by thanking Shawn and Alvaro for the privilege of allowing me to tell their story. They opened their hearts and trusted me with the most intimate details of the worst days of their young lives and, in the process, taught me the meaning of courage and grace. I cherish them both and always will.

I have had the good fortune to work with incredibly talented people. I am even more fortunate that they have been willing to share their gifts with me. *Star-Ledger* editor Jim Willse—"Mr. Willse" to me—groomed me for the best newspaper job in the world, and I am impossibly indebted to him. This book would not have been written had it not been for Fran Dauth, editor and friend, who called me into her office on a morning in January 2000 and asked if I would be interested in telling the story of the students who were burned in the Seton Hall fire. She guided the year-long project to its exalted place as the most successful series in the *Star-Ledger*'s history. Thanks doesn't begin to express my gratitude. Guy Sterling, Brian Murray, and Kelly Heyboer, your tenacious reporting on the fire investigation made all of us at the paper proud. Thank you for sharing your notes, your sources, and your expertise.

Little, Brown has been more than kind to a first-time author. Geoff Shandler believed in this book, then made it better with every stroke of his magic red pencil; and Michelle Aielli advocated for it with incessant enthusiasm.

A special thanks has to go to Saint Barnabas Medical Center in Livingston, New Jersey. Few hospitals would be willing to take the enormous risk it did of allowing a journalist in to watch high-risk patients in treatment, when death was the likely outcome. A decision was made at the highest level to allow me unfettered access to the burn unit. I believe this was done because the hospital realized that only a total cynic wouldn't recognize the wonder amid all the sorrow. Few people outside the unit would ever have known about the miracles that happen there had it not been for the hospital's public relations director, Robin Lally, and, of course, the incredible Hani Mansour and his staff, who urged the decision makers to take the risk. Thank you all for trusting me to tell the story of your extraordinary unit, and for allowing me to become part of your close-knit family. As the wonderful burn nurse Kathe Conlon told me early on: "Not everyone is accepted in the burn unit. You have to pass the test." I'm thankful I did.

I have amazing friends: Jayne Daly Munoz, Mary Romano, Kitta MacPherson Lucas, Kenny Cunningham, Marianne Timmons, Robin Boyle, thank you for believing in me.

Amy Ellis Nutt, dear amiga, few are your equal in prose, and you gave your precious time unselfishly to refine and polish mine. The value of your friendship is incalculable.

Matt Rainey, your haunting Pulitzer Prize–winning photos bring me back to those long, grueling days in the burn unit, when our working relationship blossomed into an enduring friendship.

Marilyn Dillon and Brian Horton, you inspire me.

My family is the wind in my sail. Dad, you taught me decency, drive, and determination; Carolyn, you filled a pair of shoes I thought no one could fill—my mom's; Scott, how many other brothers would read every word? You rock. Penny, on that dark day thirty-two years ago, we vowed to stick together through whatever else presented itself, and we have. You are sister and soulmate. Yvonne (Tootie), Nicole, Shawn, Emily, and Peter, my dear nieces and nephews, I couldn't love you more if . . . well, you know the rest.

Loren Fisher, the day I met you was the day the possibilities began. For eighteen years, you have shown me unconditional love, respect, and acceptance. I believe in me because you do. Now let's go to Vermont.

About the Author

Robin Gaby Fisher is a nationally acclaimed news feature writer with the *Star-Ledger* in Newark, New Jersey. She has won a National Headliner Award and the Nieman Foundation at Harvard University's Taylor Family Fairness in Media Award. She was also a member of a Pulitzer Prize–winning team and a two-time finalist for the Pulitzer Prize in feature writing. She lives with her family in New Jersey and Woodstock, Vermont. This is her first book.

BACK BAY · READERS' PICK

Reading Group Guide

After the Fire

A TRUE STORY OF FRIENDSHIP AND SURVIVAL

by

Robin Gaby Fisher

Kelly Campbell

Shawn Simons, Robin Gaby Fisher, and Alvaro Llanos on the Seton Hall campus in April 2008.

A conversation with Robin Gaby Fisher, Shawn Simons, and Alvaro Llanos

Robin, After the Fire *was developed out of an eight-part feature that you wrote for the* Newark Star-Ledger. *At what point did you realize that Shawn and Alvaro's story was a story that needed to be told and that you wanted to be the one to tell it?*

Robin: My editor at the paper, Fran Dauth, assigned me to the story. At first I was fearful. I didn't know if I could handle spending time in a burn unit. But from the moment I arrived at St. Barnabas and met the families of Shawn and Alvaro, and Dr. Mansour and his staff, I knew I wanted to stay.

Over the nine months I spent in the burn unit after the fire, I watched the story evolve from one of burn recovery to one of the courage and friendship of two very special young men. Theirs was a universal story that could benefit everyone who read it. I was proud to be the storyteller.

Who made the decision to let Robin and Matt Rainy—the photographer whose images of Shawn and Alvaro earned him a Pulitzer Prize—document your recovery? How did you get used to them being around you all the time? How did you come to trust them?

Shawn: The ultimate decision came down to Al and me, though our parents gave them the initial OK while we were still in a comatose stage. As I was the first to awaken and be told about the project, I agreed to do it only if Al agreed to be a part of the series as well.

As far as them being around all the time, it was kind of therapeutic. Besides friends and family being there, they were there often and became second sources of support, other people to talk to. They were an outlet to get things off our chest—our highlights, our low points. During this process we became friends, and I trusted that they wouldn't write or show anything that wasn't in our best interests.

Alvaro: Well, in the beginning of the accident my parents gave the OK as long as when I woke up from the coma it was my decision whether to go on with the documentation. I was used to Robin and Matt being around because they were two of the first faces I saw when I woke up from my coma, and they were there every day before I really understood what was going on. I felt comfort just having them around because I never wanted to be alone, especially when my family wasn't around.

Of the many assignments you've had, Robin, this must have been one of the more difficult to "leave at the door" every evening. What was your life like while you were writing After the Fire*?*

Robin: *After the Fire was* my life at the time. Matt Rainey was the photojournalist who worked on the newspaper story with me. We spent seven days a week reporting the story, starting early each morning and getting home late every evening. It was impossible to leave the story at the door because we came to care so very much for everyone involved. When you watch a boy struggling to live, as we did for months with Alvaro when he was teetering between life and death, you don't put it aside at night. You go to sleep with it, you dream about it, and wake up with it. And then you pray he's still alive when you get to the hospital in the morning.

After becoming personally involved with both boys and their families, how did you manage to tell the story from so many perspectives with such objectivity?

Robin: We had a pact from the beginning. In order to do such a story justice, you must record what you see and hear and edit nothing out. Everyone involved understood that. Some of the hardest parts to write were things that were the most hurtful to the boys; for instance, when Alvaro's girlfriend left him because she couldn't deal with his altered appearance. As painful as that was for Alvaro to share, he knew it was a huge component of being burned. Shawn, Alvaro, and I would talk through each of these very delicate situations. The bottom line was, we were all interested in telling the truest story we could, and sometimes that meant it was painful for everyone. Yet working through it as a team helped me to feel free to be objective.

How did you get the idea to turn the series into a book? Did changing formats alter your own experience?

Robin: The newspaper series ended with so many unanswered questions. The book came several years later when the story had come full circle. By the time of the book, the arsonists had been arrested and Shawn and Alvaro had completed their burn recovery and were getting on with their lives. We had continued our relationship so I knew what was happening with them, and I knew there was a whole new chapter of the story to be written. Newspaper stories are constrained by time and space limitations, so the book allowed me to really delve so much more into their characters and to bring the story up to date. I think it was interesting for all three of us to relive the experience together, and I know Shawn and Alvaro are really proud of their book.

What was it like to read about yourself in the third person? How closely were you involved in Robin's writing process, if at all?

Shawn: I found it both weird and amazing. Even though I lived through everything that I was reading, sometimes I forget those small details that only someone documenting me could have picked up on. Though Robin's details in her notes were extraordinary, there were still little things that needed to be tweaked or added that I would have to give to her. She constantly kept us in the loop to extra details she needed or wanted to add.

Alvaro: It was pretty cool to relive important moments of my life, and I was able to realize what my family and friends were dealing with because of my accident.

How did you feel when you first held a copy of the book?

Robin: I cried. I couldn't wait to share it with Shawn and Alvaro.

Shawn: It was incredible. To hold a piece of your life in your hand. Even though we knew the story because we lived it, to have it bound together and ready to ship was utterly amazing.

Alvaro: I thought it was pretty cool, and I felt grateful that we have a chance to inspire everyone with our story.

Which is an interesting point. As one rarely thinks of one's own experiences as being transformative for others, were you surprised by the success of After the Fire, *of its ability to move and inspire in equal measure?*

Shawn: Honestly, no. I think the story touches so many people on a personal level. Whether they attended Seton Hall or knew someone who did; had some type of affiliation with being burned or knowing someone who was; or even an affiliation with Saint Barnabas or just a New Jersey resident. It's a true story of love, commitment, courage, and inspiration. And it was written so beautifully. I have not heard from a person who has said that they wouldn't recommend this book to everyone they know. I've received numerous e-mails from strangers across the world who have found me on Facebook or MySpace to tell me how much they enjoyed the book and how inspirational it was.

Robin: I knew how touched I was by Shawn and Al and how moved I was by their story, but I think I was surprised at how many people connected with it. The response to their story has been overwhelming. Ten years after the fire, people still ask about them all the time.

What do you tell people who look to you for inspiration?

Shawn: I tell people to try to surround themselves with as much support as possible. Family and friends are the people who know you the most and will be there to support you the most. Also look for inspiration in people who might not have gone through what you have but have overcome some sort of obstacle in life.

Alvaro: I don't really have to say much; people are inspired by me before I even open my mouth. They consider me a walking miracle. They are amazed by how I carry myself with a smile and have moved on with my life. Pretty much I say each day is a blessing, and day after day life gets better.

Have any of your thoughts about the fire, its consequences, or the two boys who started it changed over the past few years?

Shawn: Not really. I've always looked at the fire as a blessing in disguise. Despite the fact that I had to endure pain and slight physical augmentations, I learned that I was strong enough to overcome this obstacle. I've met so many new people who I can truly say are friends, and I've gained a stronger emotional attachment with my family. No matter what happened to me, I still feel the most pain for the Karol, Caltabilota, and Giunta families. [*Their sons died in the fire.*] They have to live with the fact that their loved ones didn't have the chance to recover. I will never forget them.

Alvaro: Not really. I don't really think about it. I just try my best to move on with life.

Has the concept of community changed for either of you in the years since the Seton Hall fire?

Shawn: It has in the respect that the community was so responsive to the fire. The outpouring of cards and letters from everyone, from preschool children to the elderly. The respect and well wishes that people give you when they notice who you are. It has opened my heart to know that people who are complete strangers can be so supportive to individuals they have never met or possibly will never meet. Just remarkable.

Are you still in contact with the St. Barnabas nurses?

Shawn: I am somewhat, though not as much as I would like to be. It's tough when you get back to your normal life to keep in contact with all those who helped save your life. Plus there are so many nurses who have left the burn unit because one can only bear so much of seeing people suffer or not make it. I do try to make a biannual visit to see some familiar faces.

Alvaro: I try my best to go back to St. Barnabas whenever I can to say hello and give my thanks. Sometimes my physical therapist asks me to come back to speak to burn survivors so I can motivate them by having them see how far I have come along.

The three of you work together now, correct? How did this come about? Can you talk a little about the experience of working together in an office environment after sharing such an extraordinarily intimate knowledge of one another?

Robin: Shawn and Alvaro are so much a part of the newsroom it's like they have always been there. I love the fact that they work at the paper and that the paper has embraced them. Every day that I see them is a better day.

Shawn: It was kind of cosmic that we all ended up working together. After a buyout from a previous job, I thought about where I could go where people knew me already and I felt comfortable. After I talked with Robin, she said, "Why don't you come to the *Star-Ledger*?" And the rest is history.

Alvaro: It's just great to know that every day there is a chance I'm going be able to see them, because we've been through so much together.

Of the many things you learned during your time with the boys, Robin, what has proved to be the most lasting?

These boys taught me so much—about courage, about the power of friendship, about decency and kindness and spirit. My life has changed dramatically because of them, from knowing them. On my worst days, I can see one of them, or talk to them, and it all turns around to be good. I am so grateful for our enduring friendship. Shawn and Alvaro have enriched my life in so many ways. I love them and can't imagine my life without them.

This book portrays family, and the love a family can share, as an enormously powerful source of strength and courage. Do you three think of yourselves as family?

Robin: I always say Shawn and Alvaro are like nephews. I couldn't love them more if they were my immediate family.

Shawn: Without a doubt. Al and Robin have shared some of the most intimate moments of my life—milestones in my recovery, the birth of my children, holidays. There is nothing I wouldn't do for them, and I feel the same goes toward me.

Alvaro: I love Robin and Shawn; I always want them to be part of my life. They have helped me so much with the process, and with me moving on with my life. Thank you, guys.

Questions and topics for discussion

1. Why is it important for books like *After the Fire* to be written and read? Who should read this book?

2. In *After the Fire* we witness the different ways in which various people react to the initial tragedy and to the long recovery process. How do Kenny, Angie, and Daisy evolve or change over the course of the book?

3. After reading about the grueling and heartbreaking experience of being a burn doctor or nurse, were you surprised to learn that Hani Mansour and nearly all of the nurses had an extreme fear of fire and some kind of traumatic childhood experience with it? Did this information help clarify anything for you?

4. Across nine months, Fisher spent each day with Shawn, Alvaro, and their families, witnessing, at every stage, their most private moments. In your opinion, does she do a good job of presenting the story objectively? If so, can you identify some ways that she accomplished this?

5. Discuss the use of italics throughout the narrative. When do they appear and what are they meant to signify?

6. Before the fire, Shawn and Alvaro had known each other for only four months. How does their friendship develop in the course of their recovery? Do you have friends you have bonded with over extremely intense or personal experi-

ences? How do these friendships differ from other relationships you have?

7. The parents of the boys who started the fire behaved in differing ways when faced with the possibility that their sons might be in legal trouble. What did you think about how these boys' parents reacted?

8. How does Fisher build suspense and sustain narrative tension throughout *After the Fire*? How does she deal with the fact that readers may already know the outcome or details of the events related in the book?

9. There is no shortage of unforgettably moving moments in *After the Fire*. Which scenes do you remember most vividly? Which were the most shocking and difficult to read, and which were the most inspiring? Has reading *After the Fire* made you look at the world or your family differently?

LOOK FOR THESE OTHER INSPIRING STORIES IN PAPERBACK

Here If You Need Me

by Kate Braestrup

"Braestrup writes movingly, and with humor, about how she coped when her state trooper husband died in a car crash—by taking on a mission that she never imagined." —*Reader's Digest*

When a Crocodile Eats the Sun

A Memoir of Africa

by Peter Godwin

"This saga about one family's struggle in a Zimbabwe spinning apart under dictator Robert Mugabe melds political and personal history into a compelling whole. . . . Godwin offers a haunting look at the persistence of evil—and the power of family love."

—Michelle Green, *People*

A Drinking Life

A memoir by Pete Hamill

"A vivid report of a journey to the edge of self-destruction. It is tough-minded, brimming with energy, and unflinchingly honest. Mr. Hamill may lament what drink did to his memories, but to judge from this account he never lost the best of them. So instead of a monster instilling fear, alcohol in his handling becomes an obstacle to be hurdled triumphantly."

—Christopher Lehmann-Haupt, *New York Times*

Back Bay Books

Available wherever paperbacks are sold

LOOK FOR THESE OTHER INSPIRING STORIES IN PAPERBACK

The Horse Boy

A Memoir of Healing

by Rupert Isaacson

"An astonishing memoir. . . . *The Horse Boy* will leave readers with a new appreciation for autism and the healing techniques of other cultures; like Rowan, they, too, will be changed forever."

—Angela Leeper, *BookPage*

An Exact Replica of a Figment of My Imagination

A memoir by Elizabeth McCracken

"It often contains real joy and deep sorrow on the same page. . . . This is not a book about the lighter side of losing a child, it never seeks to trivialize McCracken's loss, but it does show how honesty and humor can help people survive grief, and how hearing other people's stories can make us feel less alone."

—Malena Watrous, *San Francisco Chronicle*

The Black Veil

A memoir by Rick Moody

"Compulsively readable. . . . A profound meditation on madness, shame, and history. . . . This is an enormously risky book. . . . One of the finest memoirs in recent years."

—Jeffery Smith, *Washington Post*

LOOK FOR THESE OTHER INSPIRING STORIES IN PAPERBACK

The Unwanted

A Memoir of Childhood

by Kien Nguyen

"Vivid and compelling. . . . A gripping, emotionally raw story. . . . A highly charged, episodic account of oppression, betrayal, and escape. . . . It is a story about how difficult it is to diminish the will to survive." —Richard C. Kagan, *Minneapolis Star Tribune*

Lucky

A memoir by Alice Sebold

"It's hard to believe that a book about brutal rape and its aftermath could actually be inspirational. But despite its disturbing subject, *Lucky* is exhilarating to read." —Francine Prose, *Elle*

Another Season

A Coach's Story of Raising an Exceptional Son

by Gene Stallings and Sally Cook

"By explaining the challenge and heartbreak of raising a son with Down syndrome—while at the same time coaching a national championship team—*Another Season* rises to the level of grand autobiography." —Winston Groom, author of *Forrest Gump*

Back Bay Books
Available wherever paperbacks are sold